AF604774

ICONIC CHAPPELL

THE MAKING OF A LEGEND IN 50 IMAGES

The unauthorized collection

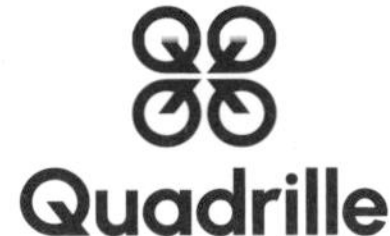

Quadrille

‘IF IT’S NOT BOLD, IF IT’S NOT RUFFLING FEATHERS, WHAT’S THE POINT?’[1]

INTRODUCTION

Anyone who has heard the opening bars of Chappell Roan's sleeper hit 'Pink Pony Club' will be familiar with that feeling: a sense of anticipation and a build-up of joy. And then the exquisite vocals begin. By the time the catchy, upbeat chorus has kicked in, you're dancing.

From her earliest beginnings in the Bible Belt of the US to her rise to global fame as one of the most iconic popstars on the planet, it's been one hell of a ride for Chappell Roan. You may be a die-hard fan who has been there since her earliest YouTube videos and first coffee-shop gigs, or one of the legions of adoring listeners who stream her songs and pack out her concerts now. One thing is for certain: there's nobody quite like Chappell Roan. With her immaculate drag-inspired make-up, foot-high bouffant wigs and dazzling array of creative costumes, she always puts on an unforgettable show – and that's before she's even opened her mouth. She's responsible for some of the most interesting and exciting songs released in the last few years, and as her star has risen, the world has started to sit up and take notice.

With fans including Elton John and Olivia Rodrigo, and a love of glitter that could keep craft shops the world over in business for decades, let's get to know this icon a little better. It's time to meet Chappell Roan.

BEGINNINGS

The earliest years of the Midwest Princess

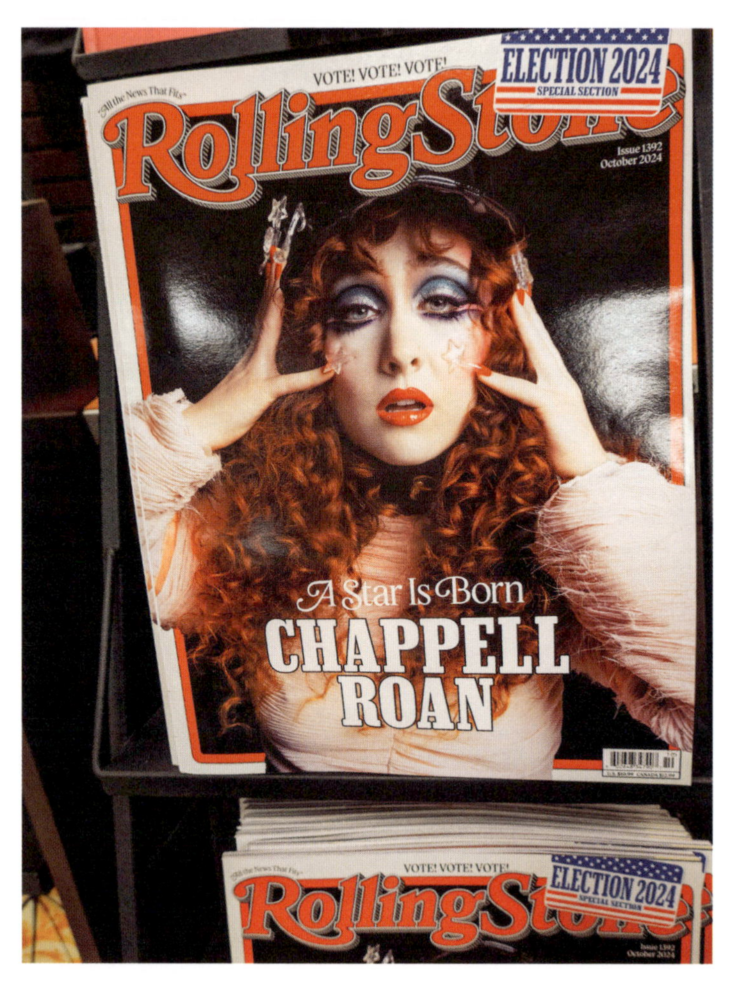
"All the News That Fits"
VOTE! VOTE! VOTE!
ELECTION 2024
SPECIAL SECTION
Issue 1392
October 2024
A Star Is Born
CHAPPELL
ROAN

A (FUTURE) STAR IS BORN

On 19 February 1998, Kayleigh Rose Amstutz was born. Her parents, Dwight and Kara, were just twenty-three when they had her. She's the oldest of four kids, and her mother works as a vet, while her dad is a nurse.

She grew up in the small town of Willard, Missouri, which has a population of around 6,500 (that's far fewer people than now attend some of her concerts).

'I'm from the Bible Belt,' Chappell told *Polyester* magazine in 2023. 'There's a lot of churches and a lot of straight people with families and it's just really encouraged [for women] to take on the role of wife and mother. There's this mentality that a woman should be a princess, but also she should be a cook, a cleaner, a driver and so on. I never fit into that mould. I really, really tried.'[2] Still, she says, 'the Midwest remains a very big part of who I am. It's where I grew up and I do love certain parts of it.'

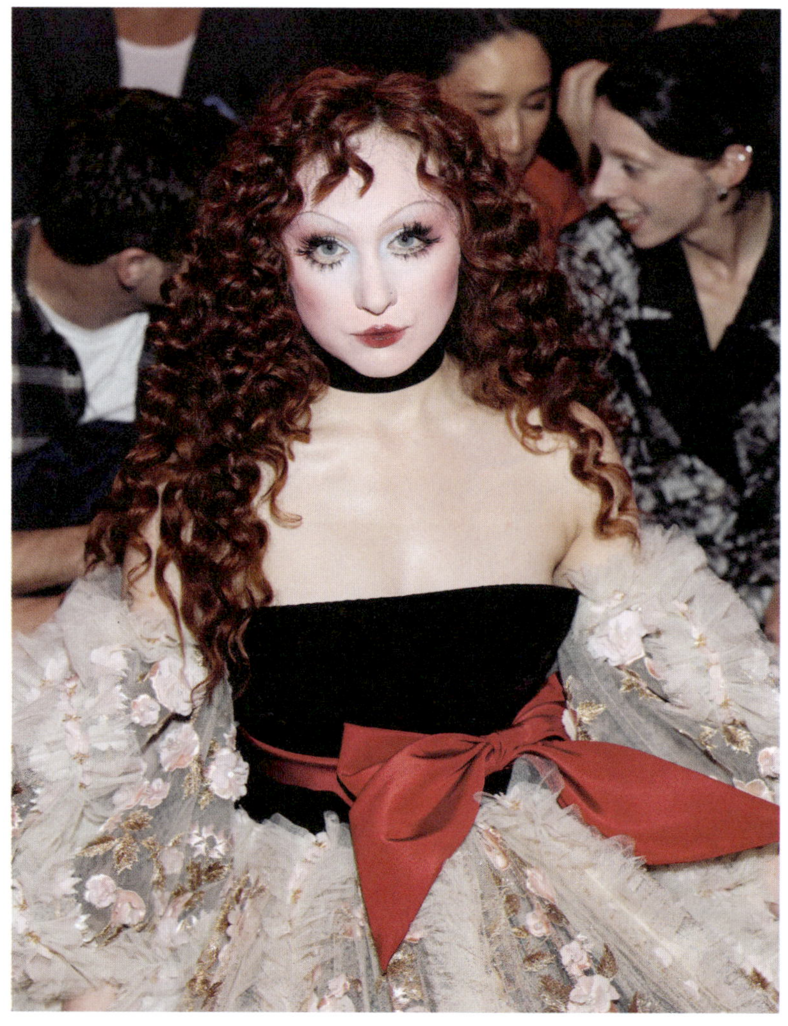

GROWING UP IN THE BIBLE BELT

As a child, Chappell (or Kayleigh, as she was known then), went to church three times a week and attended Christian summer camps. Describing one of these camps to *Vanity Fair*, Chappell said it was 'not it', adding: 'It was like, go to camp, learn Bible verses, have a fun game? Worship, go swimming, eat dinner, worship again. Go to sleep and pray.'[3]

In a 2023 interview with *Nylon*, Chappell revealed that she's known she is queer since the seventh grade: 'I was just like, girls are so pretty.'[4] But growing up in a small, conservative town, her queerness wasn't something she yet felt able to acknowledge openly, as she explained in an interview with the *Guardian*: 'I pushed down the gay part of myself so deep because I was like, that can't possibly be me!'[5]

She was a keen runner and competed at state level. In another life, she might have gone to college for cross country (though thank goodness she didn't, because we'd have missed out on so much incredible music). She made her own clothes and was something of a loner, struggling with mental health issues. 'I felt so miserable for my whole childhood,' she told *Rolling Stone* in 2024. 'All my parents could do was try their best.'[6] Later, she'd learn she had been living with bipolar disorder (see page 97).

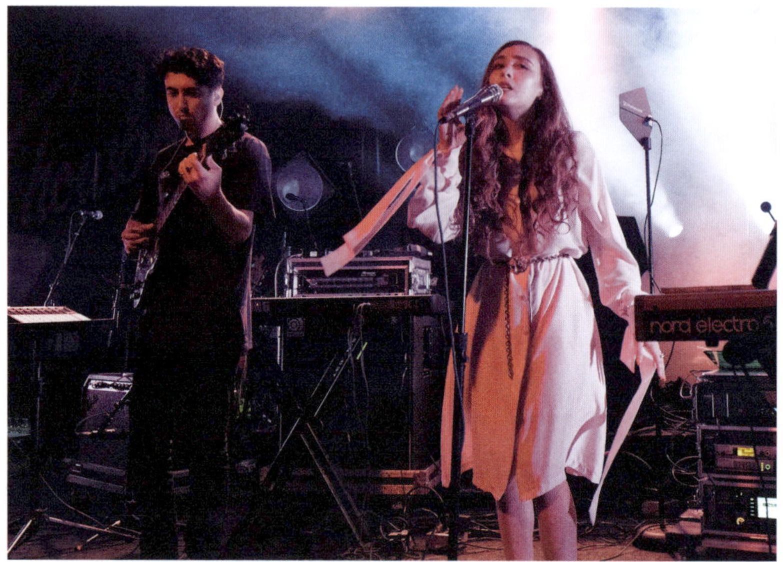

DISCOVERING MUSIC

Gradually, she began to discover her own taste in music. In an interview with *NME*, she explained: 'I was raised on Christian rock, but I never identified with it. I felt such a push and a pull because I was so curious about pop music but couldn't identify why I related to it. It was [talking about] a lifestyle I did not live. I was very sheltered and very prude.'[7]

Perhaps that's why the young Kayleigh was so shocked the first time she saw the music video for Lady Gaga's 'Alejandro'. She later told the *Guardian*: 'I was like, "Oh my god, is this porn?"'[8]

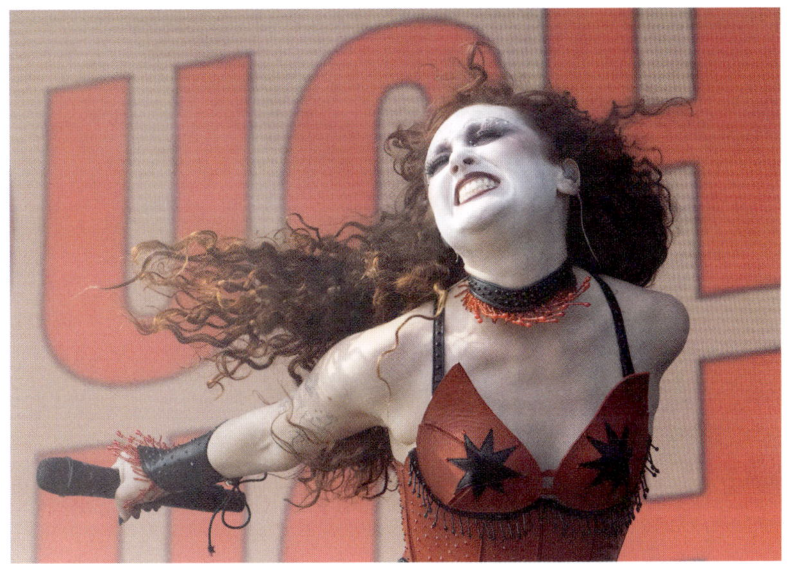

NEVER ONE TO PLAY BY THE RULES

Despite being shy and somewhat prudish, there were some early signs that this was a girl whose creativity would refuse to be constrained by rules and expectations. In an interview with *Illustrate Magazine*, Chappell revealed: 'I took piano lessons for a few years, but refused to learn theory because it was too boring.'[9] Instead, she learned by ear and copied her piano teacher's hand movements. She also took vocal lessons, but avoided a classical approach, explaining she was more interested in learning 'how to really belt and sing with confidence'. Those lessons sure paid off.

TALENT SHOWS AND TEENAGE WOES

When she was thirteen years old, the young Kayleigh took part in her school talent show, singing 'The Christmas Song'. She won – and then won again the following year. As those around her started to realise she had a real talent, she was still trying to work out who she was – and what her sound would be.

Reflecting on what she was like at that age, Chappell told *Rolling Stone*: 'I was just a freak and really shy and self-conscious and modest … The pendulum really swung so far when I started writing pop music because I was like, "I have to do my inner child justice and just be free."'[10]

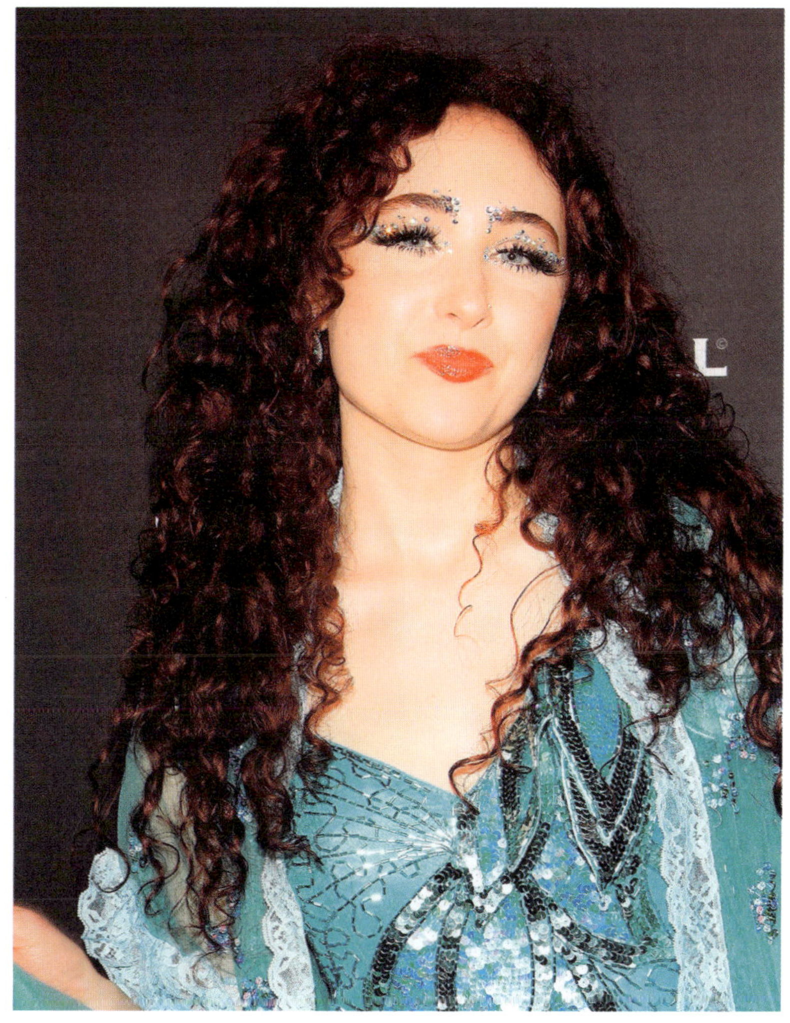

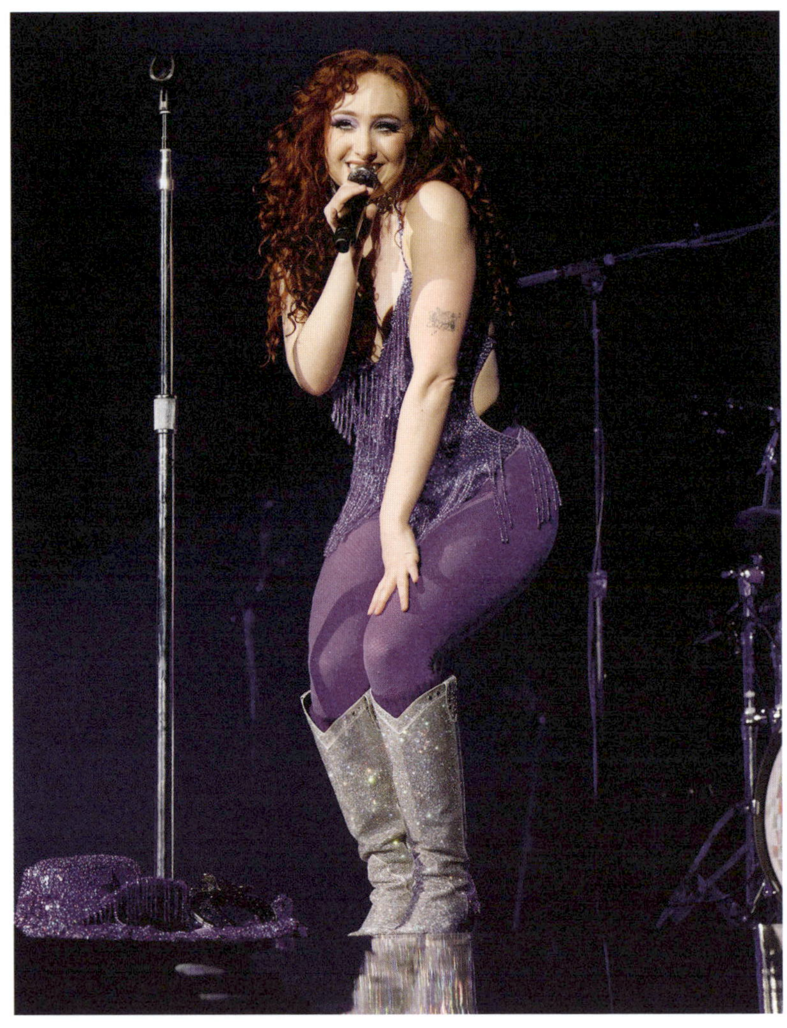

FIRST LOVE, FIRST SONG

In her teens, Kayleigh began making her initial forays into songwriting. Her first creation was inspired by her crush on an older Mormon boy she knew from school. The boy in question was about to go away on his mission (a period young Mormons usually spend away from home, volunteering and encouraging others to join their faith). Faced with his imminent departure, she felt like she 'had to write the greatest love song of all time'. What she came up with was – in her own words – 'a boring ballad'.[11]

So the song didn't work out – and neither did things with the boy. 'He was such an asshole,' Chappell explained in a 2024 interview.[12] No great loss, then.

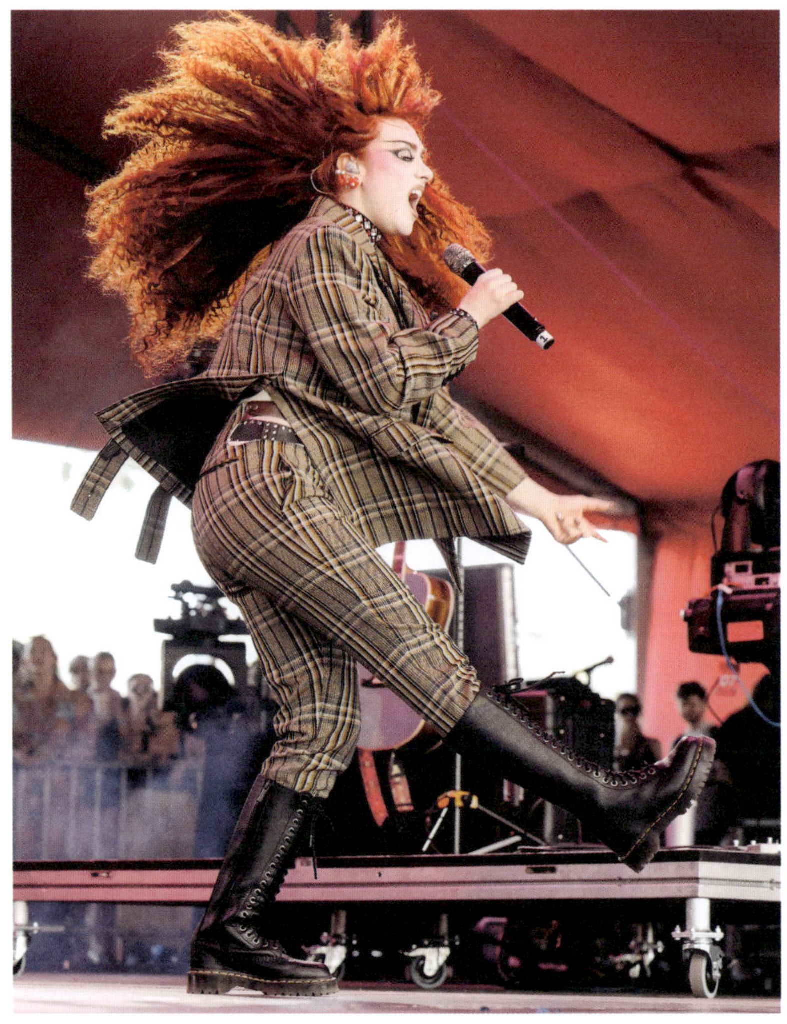

SUMMER CAMP SUPERSTAR

After her less-than-favourable impression of church camp, Chappell Roan fans can breathe a sigh of relief that she decided to give summer camp another go – this time attending a music camp at the Interlochen Center for the Arts, Michigan. While she was there, she wrote the song 'Die Young'. The camp's songwriting instructor, Seth Bernard, was blown away by the young singer, telling Pridesource.com: 'She knocked me out immediately.'[13]

Speaking to *Vanity Fair* about the experience, Chappell said: 'I felt like it was the first time I'd ever been around creative kids. Like, truly people who were passionate about writing poems and being emotional. I just didn't have that growing up … I had so many people at camp that I felt like I belonged. [I realised] there are people out there that think and feel like me.'[14]

RISE AND FALL

Her first foray into the music industry – and the birth of Chappell Roan.

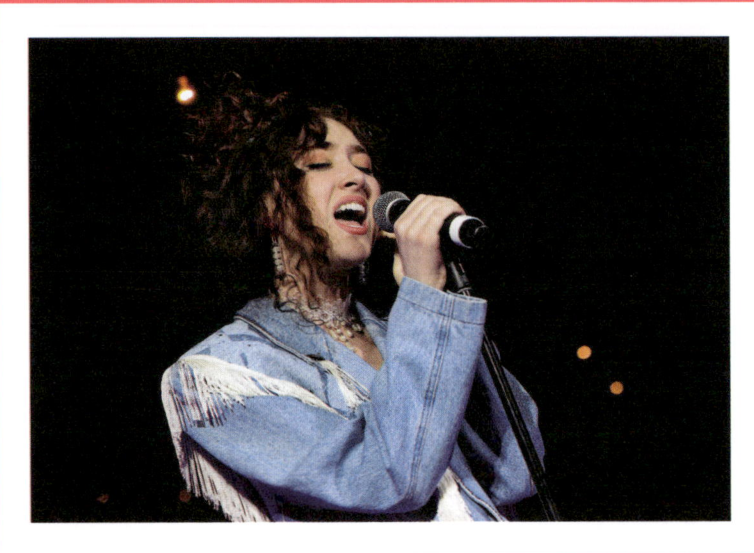

'I'M ABOUT THIRTY PER CENT KAYLEIGH ON THE STAGE. BUT IF I'M DOING A SONG LIKE "KALEIDOSCOPE", THEN I'M FULLY KAYLEIGH.'[15]

ATLANTIC CALLING

On 8 May 2015, Kayleigh signed to Atlantic Records. In a 2024 interview with Jimmy Fallon, Chappell shared the story of how her record deal was announced during her school's morning updates, just before the lunch specials: 'Yeah … it was in the same sentence.'[16]

At such a young age, signing with a major label must have been a dizzying experience. 'I was seventeen and I thought I was gonna win a Grammy,' she later told the *Guardian*. 'It's funny, because when you sign to a label, that's when the real work begins.'[17]

The music she was working on at the time felt quite different to the vibrant, anthemic pop we associate with her today. Reflecting on these changes, Chappell told the BBC in 2024: 'I feel like I moulted out of an old skin and I'm a new woman! I'm not that teenage girl anymore, but she's the reason I am where I am now.'[18]

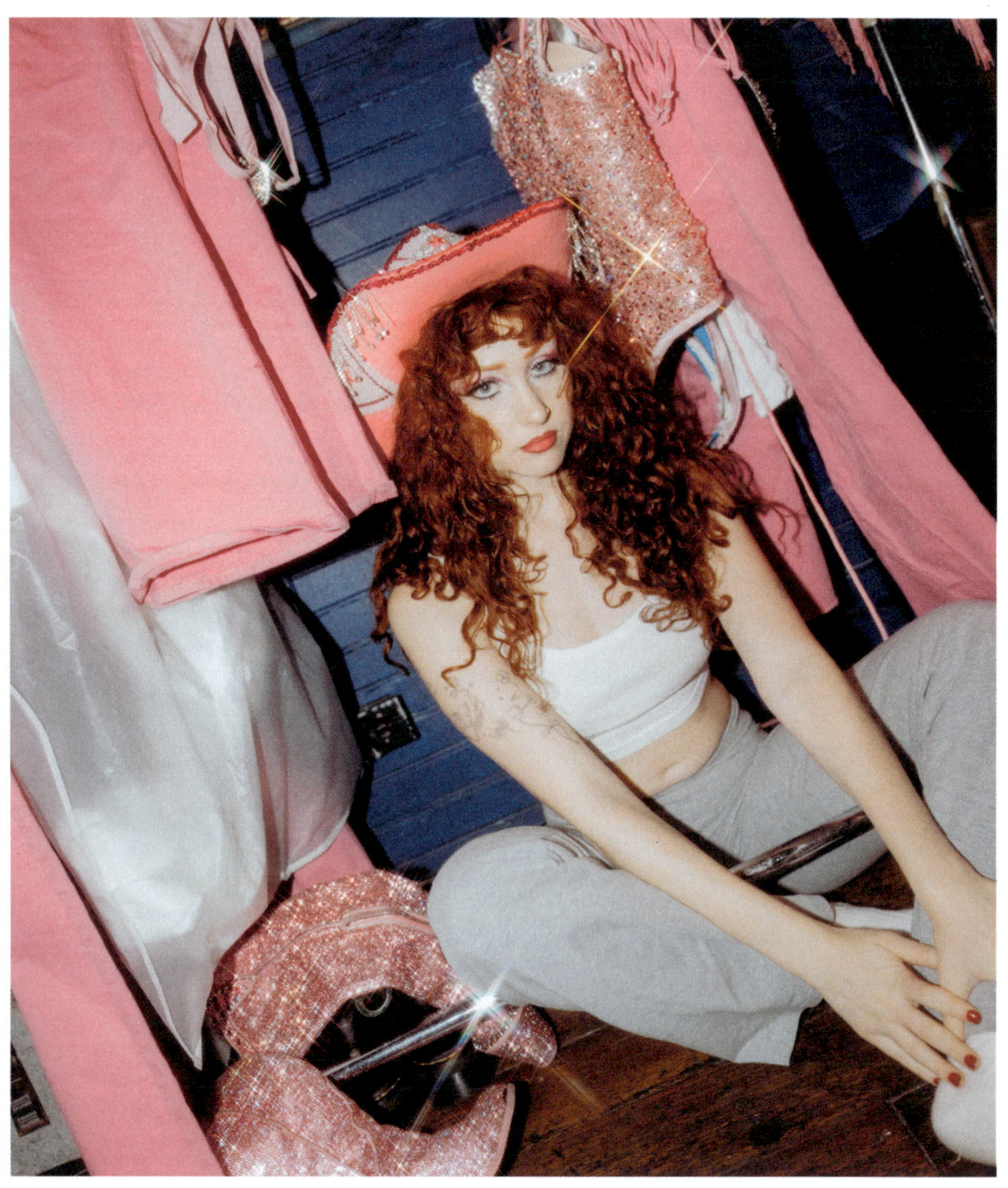

BECOMING CHAPPELL ROAN

In 2016, Kayleigh Rose Amstutz adopted the stage name Chappell Roan – and an icon was created. In an interview with Cherwell.org, she explained, 'I have never felt super connected to my real name, Kayleigh.'[19] Picking a new moniker wasn't easy, though. 'Honestly, picking my name was the hardest out of everything,' she told *Unclear Magazine*, 'because it's like … you're stuck with it once you pick it. We went through – I'm not kidding – literally thousands of names, and I always kept coming back to Chappell.'[20]

That's because it's a family name, honouring her late grandfather, Dennis K. Chappell – while the 'Roan' references his favourite song, 'The Strawberry Roan' by Curley Fletcher. It's a beautiful story and, she says, 'a very sentimental name. I do still wish my name was not Kayleigh in real life, though.'[21]

For those in any doubt about how to pronounce it, Chappell has made it crystal clear. She was captured on video pausing mid-show, resplendent in a shimmering leotard, and explaining firmly, 'If you've been saying "Shapelle Rowe-Ann", this is your final warning. It's "Chappell Roan", babe.'[22]

That's 'Chappell' as in 'chapel' and 'Roan' to rhyme with 'bone'. So now you know.

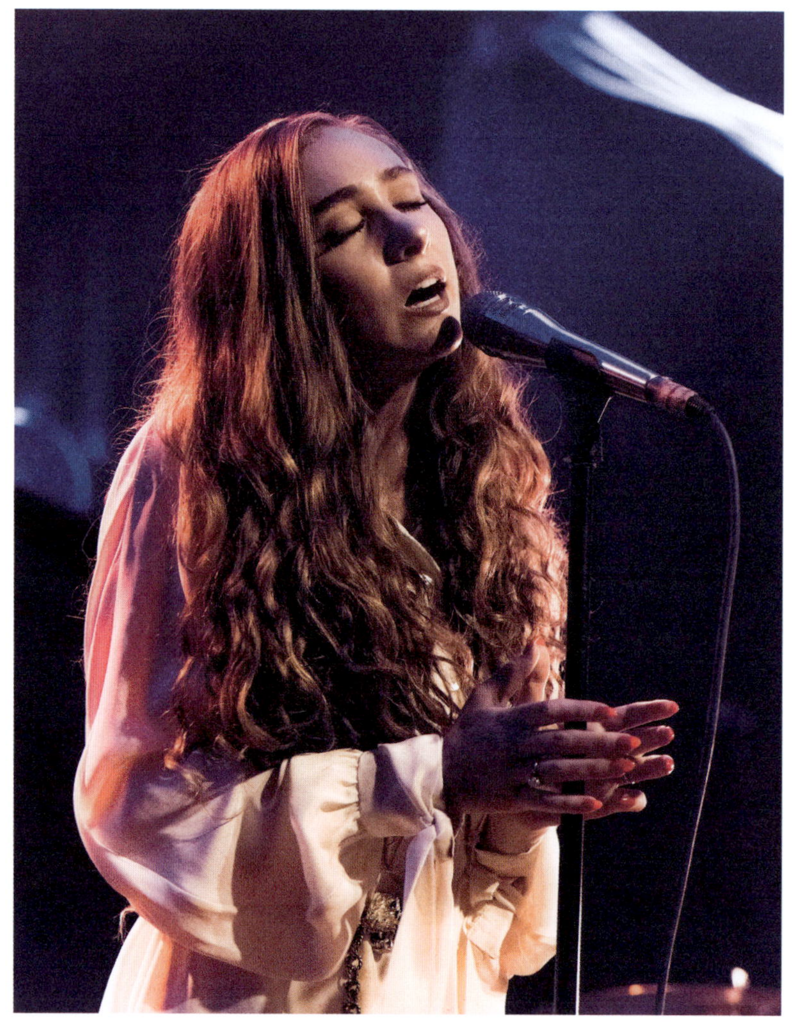

SCHOOL NIGHTS

In 2017, Chappell Roan's debut EP was released. It was entitled *School Nights*, which is perhaps a little ironic given that she'd missed her senior year at high school, including prom and graduation, to write and record it, commuting back and forth between Missouri and LA. Although the sound was still some way away from the soaring, synthy anthems her fans have come to love, her experiences visiting LA were starting to spark real changes for the young Chappell.

When she first visited, she was nervous. She'd grown up in the Bible Belt, remember, and later told *NME*: 'I was told this city is demonic and Satanists live here … But when I got to West Hollywood, it opened my eyes [to the fact] that everything I was afraid of wasn't always true.'[23]

Now, she says, she adores West Hollywood: 'I feel allowed to be who I want to be here.'[24]

A GAME-CHANGING GAY BAR

In 2018, Chappell made her first visit to a gay bar – The Abbey in West Hollywood – and it was a revelation for her. She told the *Guardian*: 'I grew up thinking being gay was bad and a sin … [Then] I went to the gay club once and it was so impactful, like magic. It was the opposite of everything I was taught.'[25]

In another interview with the BBC, Chappell explained: 'I know how cliché this sounds, but I walked into that club … and it was like heaven. It was amazing to see all these people who were happy and confident in their bodies and wearing risqué things. And the Go-Go dancers! I was enthralled.'[26]

It's easy to see the huge impact that life-changing evening had on Chappell, from the stunning outfits she wears to her tireless commitment to supporting the LGBTQ+ community. Ultimately, that night at The Abbey was the inspiration behind her spectacular song 'Pink Pony Club'.

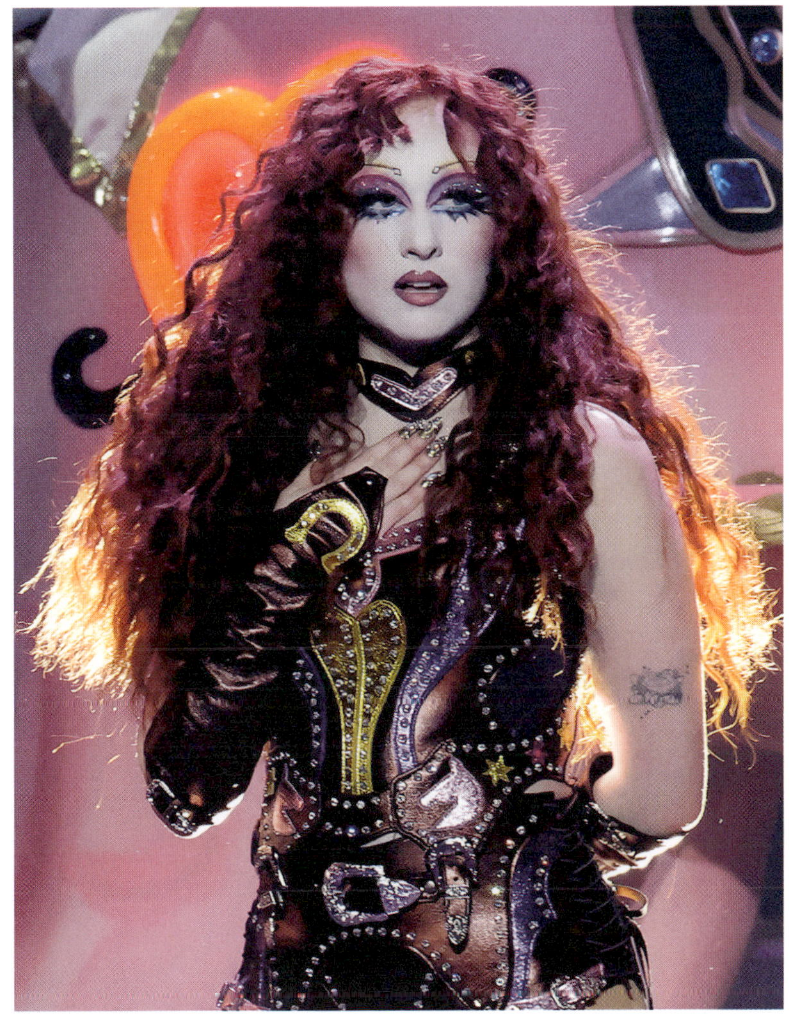

PINK PONY CLUB

In April 2020, 'Pink Pony Club' was released, marking a new and exciting sound for Chappell Roan. Unfortunately, it seemed like the world – or perhaps her record label – wasn't quite ready for this now-iconic song. The single went largely unnoticed – although more than a year later, *Vulture* proclaimed it the 'song of the summer', declaring: 'Summer 2020 just wasn't ready, but this one belongs to the Pink Pony Girls.'[27]

Vulture might have been a year late to the Pink Pony party, but it turns out they were still miles ahead of everyone else – including Atlantic, as we'll see.

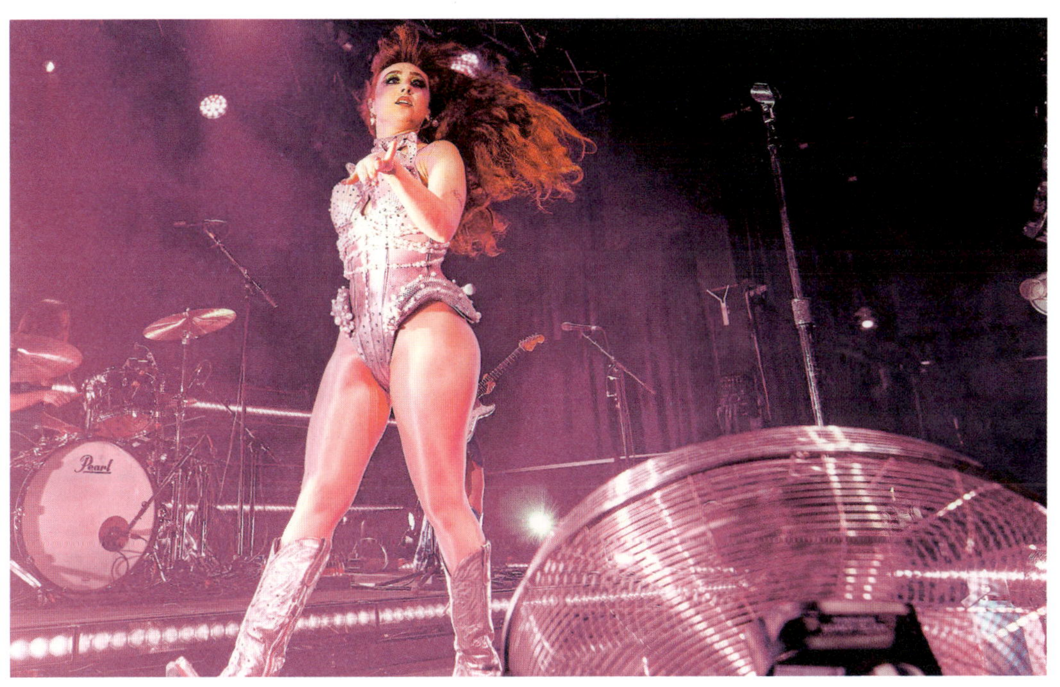
Pearl

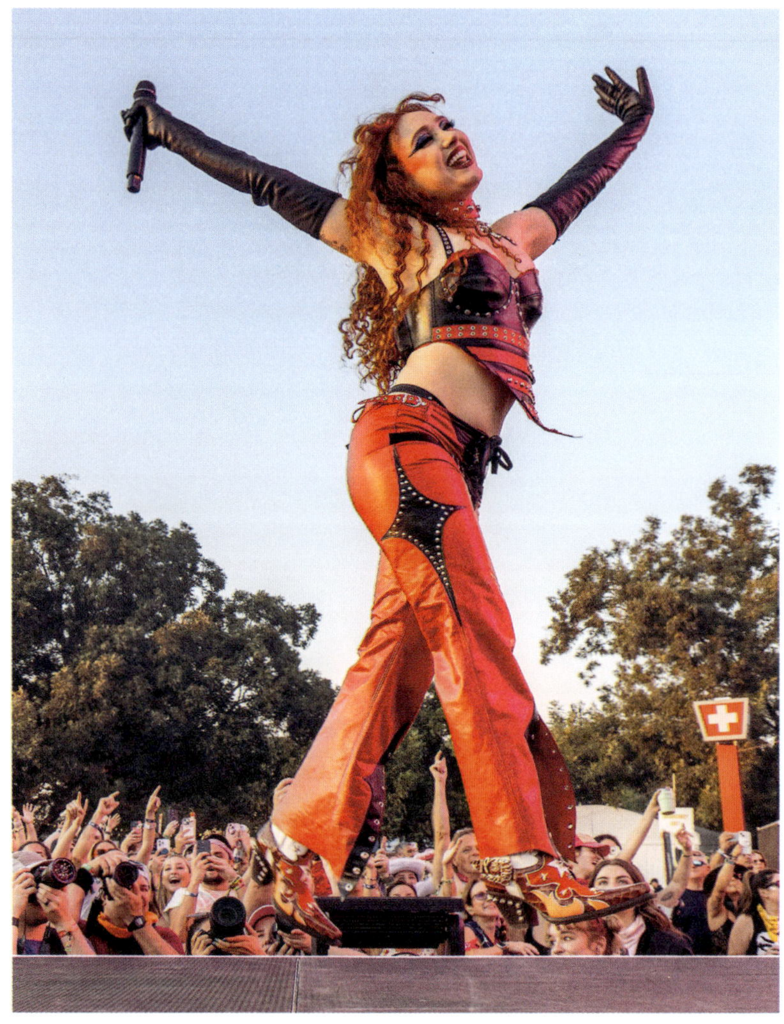

THE DROP

Soon after the release of 'Pink Pony Club', Atlantic dropped Chappell Roan. To say it was 'their loss' would be an understatement – it's easy to imagine there are some very red faces in that record label boardroom now.

Being dropped from the label was devastating for the young Chappell. 'I felt like a failure, but I knew deep down I wasn't,'[28] she later told the *Guardian*.

That deep-rooted sense that she was onto something is what got Chappell through the next year or two. In an interview with *Rolling Stone*, she explained: '[Atlantic] weren't just a little wrong. They were really, really wrong. To know that my gut instinct was right is the best feeling in the world. Purposeful revenge does not feel good, but revenge by accident feels awesome.'[29]

Despite the blow of losing her record deal and the uncertainty around her future, Chappell decided to keep on dancing (and singing).

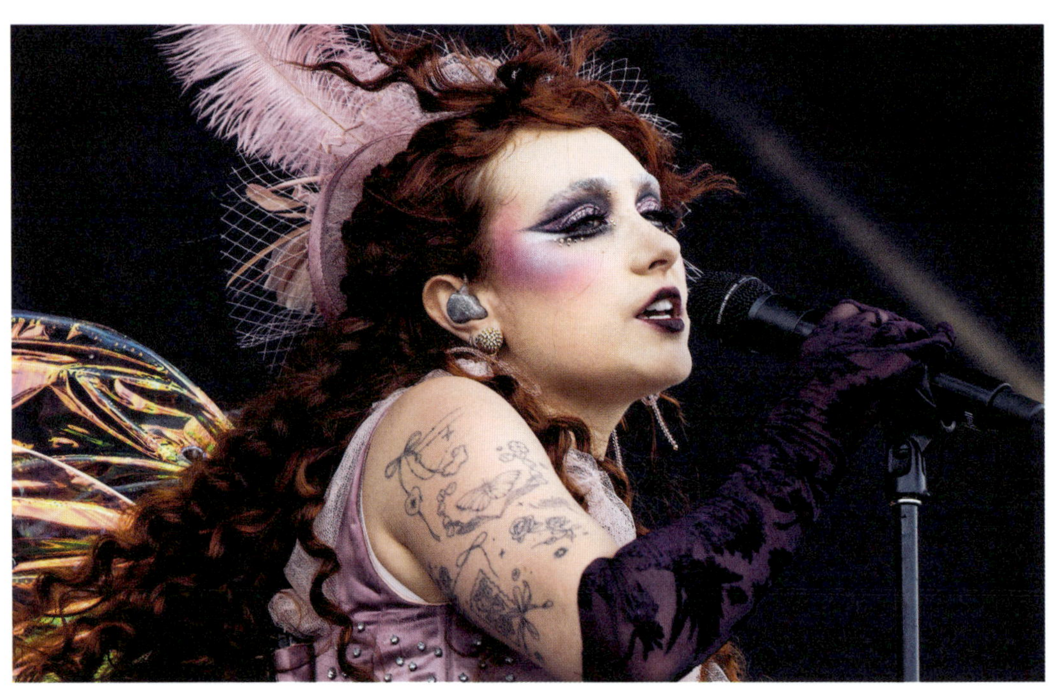

'I'M GONNA GIVE IT A YEAR'

Chappell returned home to Missouri and started working as a barista and a nanny, as well as taking shifts behind the counter in a doughnut shop – but all the while, she was figuring out what she'd do next.

Before long, she realised that what she needed to do was move back to LA. She explained to *Vanity Fair*: 'It felt like I needed to get out of Missouri to finish the rest of the songs that needed to be written. I couldn't write pop songs while I was depressed on a farm.'[30]

This meant working several jobs and taking on a DIY approach to see if she could make music work. 'I was working the drive-through and I would just think of little song melodies and write on my Notes app. And that's kind of how I kept the flame going.'[31]

Without the backing of a record label, Chappell had to get creative. She told *NME*: 'I was the thrift-store pop girl. It was so drag. I learned to embellish my own costumes. I was like, "I'm gonna give it one more year – and if it doesn't work, I'll rethink." But do you know what, it fucking worked.'[32]

Hell yes, it did.

THE COMEBACK TO END ALL COMEBACKS

Chappell makes a bold new start – on her own terms.

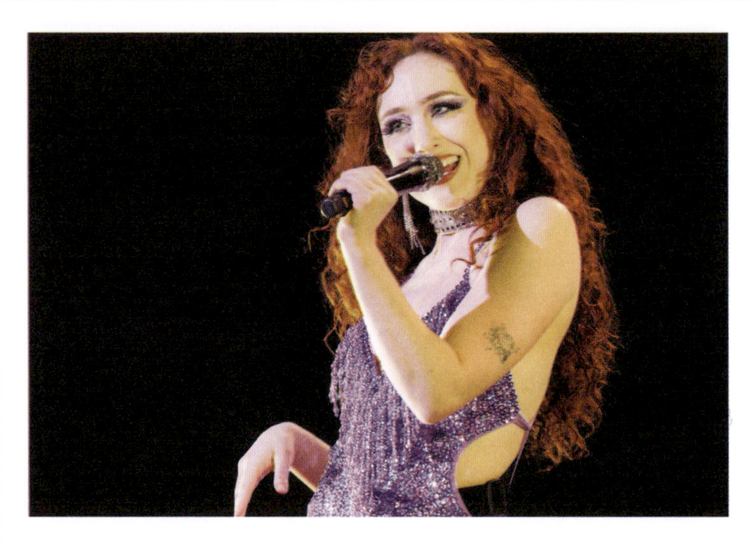

'I JUST WANTED TO MAKE SOMETHING THAT I COULD PARTY TO AND OTHER PEOPLE COULD PARTY TO.'[33]

INDEPENDENT WOMAN

In early 2022, Chappell signed with Sony – this time, instead of a record deal, she signed a publishing deal. This gave her more flexibility and freedom to develop her style, but meant that she was still essentially an independent artist, trying to write songs and build a fan base on her own. She reconnected with producer and songwriter Dan Nigro, with whom she'd collaborated while still with Atlantic. Free from constraints and eager to push boundaries, the pair started exploring the new sound they'd hit upon with 'Pink Pony Club'. Something big was brewing.

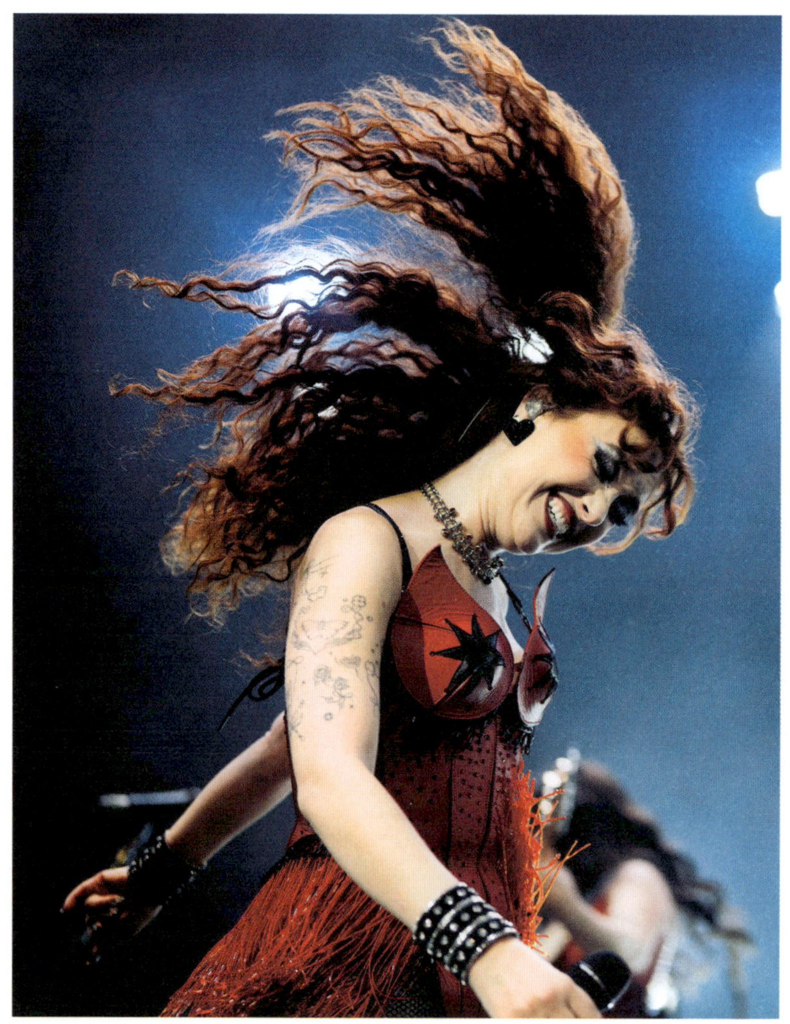

NAKED IN MANHATTAN

On 18 February 2022, Chappell released her first new music in two years: the single 'Naked in Manhattan', which she'd worked on with Nigro. It was her first time releasing a song without the backing of a label. The music video – featuring a pink stiletto-shaped phone, glittering outfits and Chappell dancing through New York City streets in a prom-style red gown – also gives a brief glance of her lower-back 'Princess' tattoo.

In a TikTok video shared ahead of the song's release, Chappell explained: 'I wrote this song about my first queer experience. I tried to capture how truly amazing it was in a pop song.'[34] In a comment underneath the video, she added: 'I started tearing up posting this. It really doesn't feel real.'

Packed with references to *Mean Girls*, Lana Del Rey and slumber parties, the song's evocative and lingering exploration of sexuality made one thing abundantly clear: Chappell Roan was back, and this time, she wasn't taking orders from anyone.

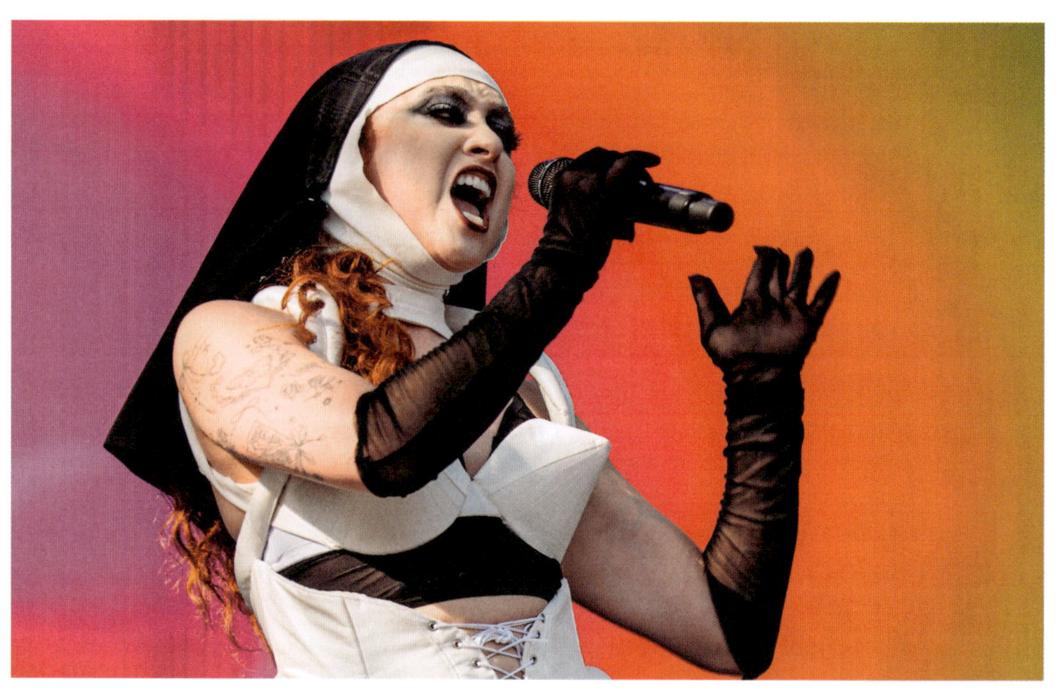

MY KINK IS KARMA

Just a couple of months later – and with a buzz beginning to grow around the bold new sound Chappell was sharing – she followed up with another single release. 'My Kink is Karma' was unleashed on 6 May 2022. The song is an unashamed acknowledgement of that sickly-sweet sense of satisfaction you get when you realise that your ex's life is going up in flames. In an interview with *Into*, Chappell shared: 'I've been through some pretty gnarly break-ups. I was just sitting in the session and I was like, "Ah, it feels so nice that my ex is doing horrible!" Which is insanely toxic. The song is toxic. I'm very aware that it's not healthy. But that's how I was feeling that day.'[35]

The song was accompanied by a striking music video featuring Chappell – wearing red lingerie and devil horns, with her face painted in a white heart shape – taunting an ex whose own face is daubed with clown make-up. It's like a revenge fantasy come to life, complete with a throbbing synth and unforgettable hook.

SWEET AND SOUR

On 27 May 2022 (the night after her own first headline show in LA), Chappell opened for Olivia Rodrigo in San Francisco as part of Rodrigo's Sour Tour. Rodrigo had also worked with Dan Nigro, and Chappell had provided backing vocals for some of her tracks, including 'Lacy' and 'Can't Catch Me Now'. Rodrigo was eager to help get Chappell's music out there – and the show was a huge success.

Dressed in a hot pink outfit, Chappell performed for thousands of screaming fans, who joined in enthusiastically with songs including 'Naked in Manhattan' and 'My Kink is Karma'. The next day, Chappell wrote on Instagram: 'This was fucking crazy. Thank you @oliviarodrigo for asking me to open. It was truly an honor. Your fans were the sweetest angels to me.'[36]

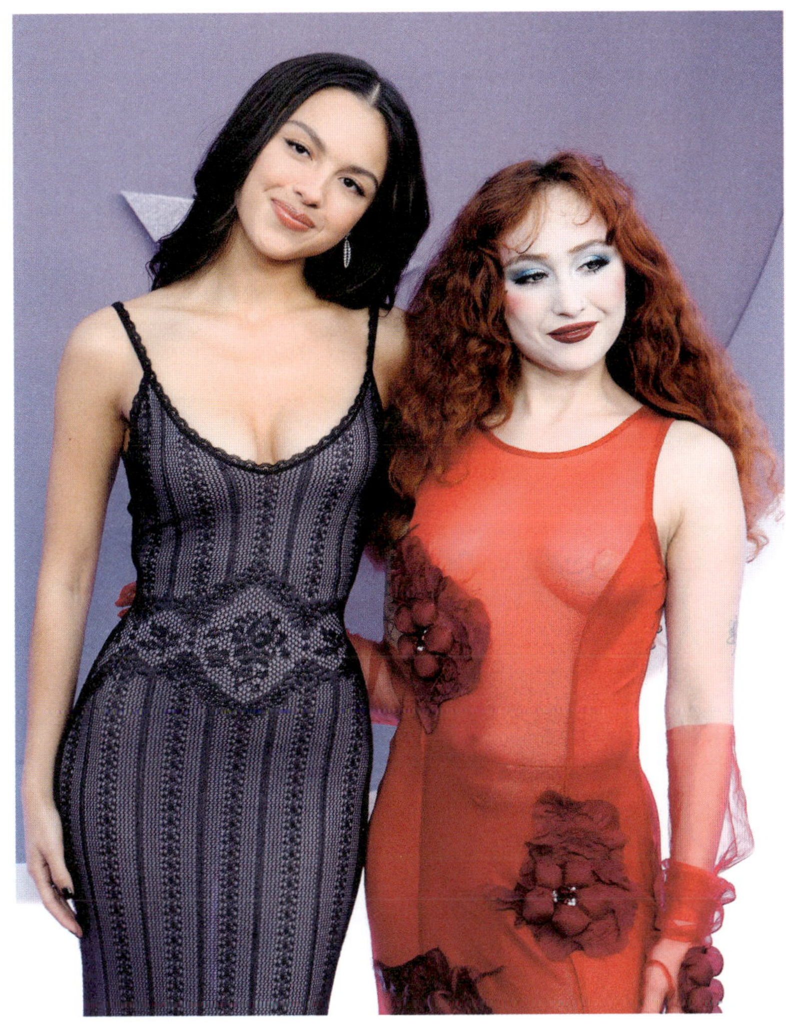

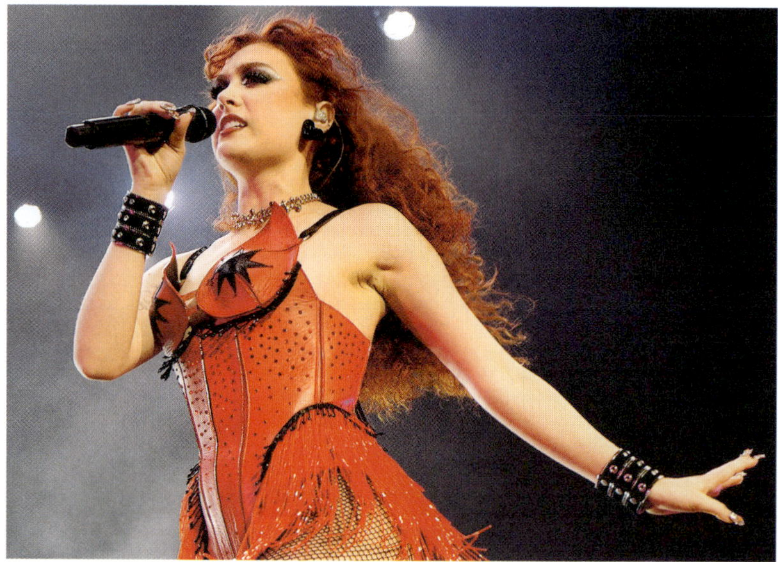

IT'S A FEMININOMENON

On 12 August 2022, Chappell showed she wasn't afraid of tongue-twisters when she released her next single, 'Femininomenon' (which is hard to say, let alone sing). The song opens with soft, dreamy vocals and a gentle pace, before rapidly descending into a dramatic, playful anthem that fizzes with energy and allows Chappell's vibrant personality to come across. The music video shows her dancing about wearing vampire fangs and tearing around fields on a dirt bike dressed in hot pink chaps. In an Instagram post just ahead of the song's release, Chappell wrote: 'Thank you to my sweet father who let me bedazzle his dirt bike.'[37]

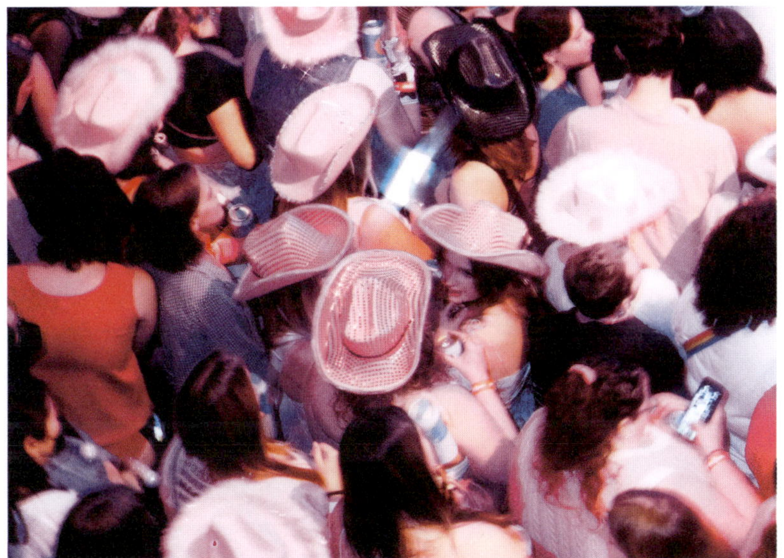

HEADLINE ACT

Chappell's star was slowly but surely on the rise. August 2022 saw her play two key headline shows: one at the iconic New York venue the Bowery Ballroom, and another at the Troubadour in West Hollywood. Announcing fancy dress themes for each show, she invited New York fans to wear outfits inspired by 'My Kink is Karma', while the West Hollywood theme, fittingly enough, was 'Pink Pony Club'. Following the West Hollywood show, Chappell wrote on Instagram: 'I got home last night and cried. I'm so grateful for each and every one of you who helped this come to life. The pink pony club officially exists.'[38]

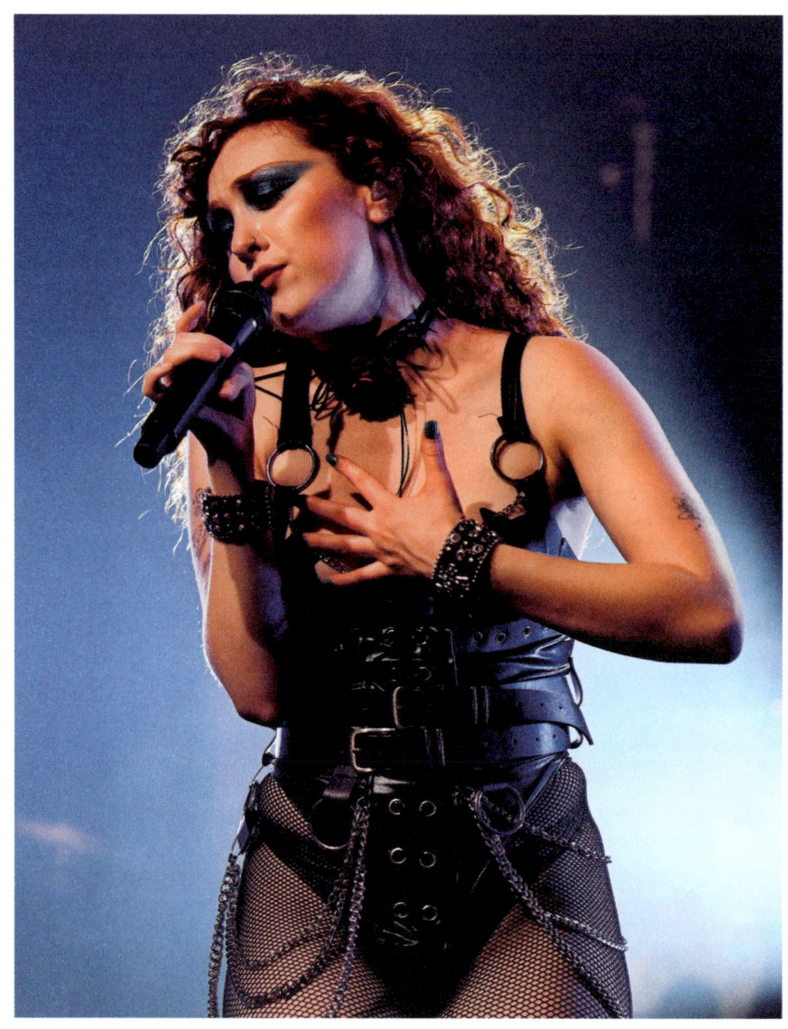

CASUAL

On 28 October 2022, Chappell released 'Casual', a swoon-worthy country-style ballad with biting lyrics. The song was inspired by the painful end of a relationship that had been intense and important for her – yet was, she discovered, described by the other person as 'casual'. In an interview with *Rolling Stone*, Chappell said: '[T]hey had told my friend it was nothing and it was just casual. And in my head I was like, "What the fuck do you mean it was casual? We were telling secrets and talking literally every day!"'

The single was accompanied by a simple 'visualiser' video featuring Chappell singing and crafting in a bedroom, wearing blue and green fairy wings. The melancholic yet beautiful vocals saw the song gather traction on TikTok, where it went viral.

In March of the following year, the official music video was released: a sumptuously shot, cinematic dreamscape in which Chappell falls for a siren who emerges from the waves, but ultimately breaks her heart.

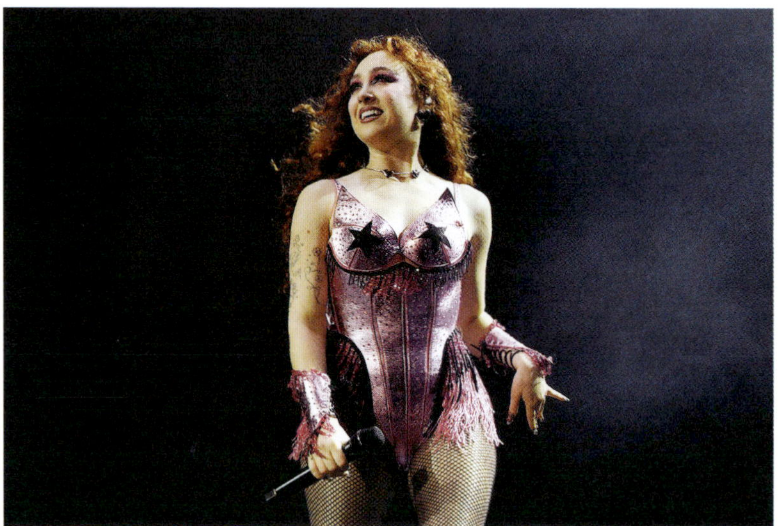

NAKED IN NORTH AMERICA

In November 2022, Chappell announced a headline tour for early 2023 entitled *Naked in North America*. Within days of the announcement, most of the shows had sold out and others had to be upgraded to larger venues. By the time the tour rolled around, every single date had sold out.

The tour kicked off on 15 February in Phoenix and ended on 15 March in LA. Each date was given its own theme, from 'Goth, grunge and glitter' to 'Rhinestones and rainbows'. Every show was opened by a local drag act, highlighting Chappell's links to the queer community and her love of the drag aesthetic.

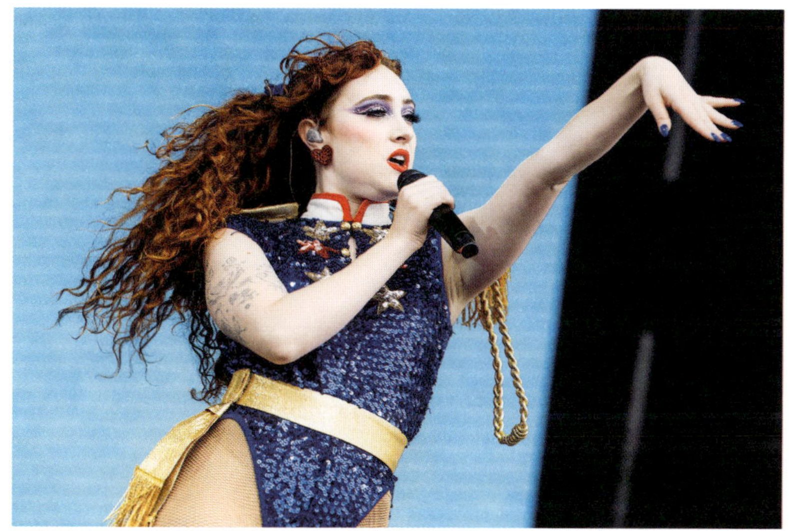

NEW RECORD DEAL, WHO DIS?

In May 2023, after three years as an independent artist, Chappell signed a record deal with Island Records as part of Dan Nigro's Amusement Records imprint. In an interview with Grammy.com, she explained: 'I ended up signing [with them] because this project honestly got too big to be independent anymore.'

She needed to do things *her* way. Luckily, Island Records seemed to be on board with that. As she told *The Face* magazine: 'I probably have one of the best deals ... because I was like, "Fuck you guys, give me what I want or I'll do it myself" ... Now I can be like, "Look at the numbers, bitch."'[39]

RISE AND ... RISE

After her years of hard work and dedication,
Chappell is catapulted to fame.

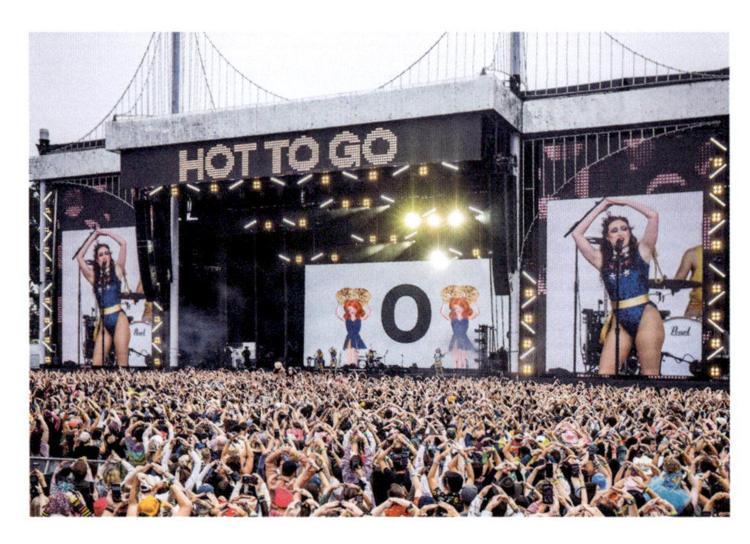

'AS THE PROJECT GROWS, I CAN DO BIGGER SHOWS AND BE LIKE, "I WANT OUTFIT CHANGES NOW," AND, "I WANT MORE LIGHTS," AND, "I WANT CONFETTI." I CAN AFFORD CONFETTI NOW!'[40]

HOT TO GO, GO, GO

The singles kept coming thick and fast, each one gaining more and more of a buzz: there was the ethereal, otherworldly beauty of 'Kaleidoscope' in March 2023, followed by the fizzingly magical 'Red Wine Supernova' in May. For many Chappell fans, though, it was August's electropop banger 'HOT TO GO!' that really kicked things up a notch, with its catchy, playful chorus and 'YMCA'-style dance routine. In an interview with *Vanity Fair*, Chappell explained that the inspiration for the song, and its accompanying dance, was simple: 'I wanted to be a cheerleader so bad because I always thought they were just so cool and so hot and, I don't know, they were just so sassy at my school. And so it's ... dream-come-true vibes.'[41]

For the music video, Chappell returned to Missouri and brought her brand of zingy fresh pop home to the Midwest. She even taught her grandparents the iconic dance so they could appear with her in the video. She reflected: 'They're just really proud of me and they always have been.'[42]

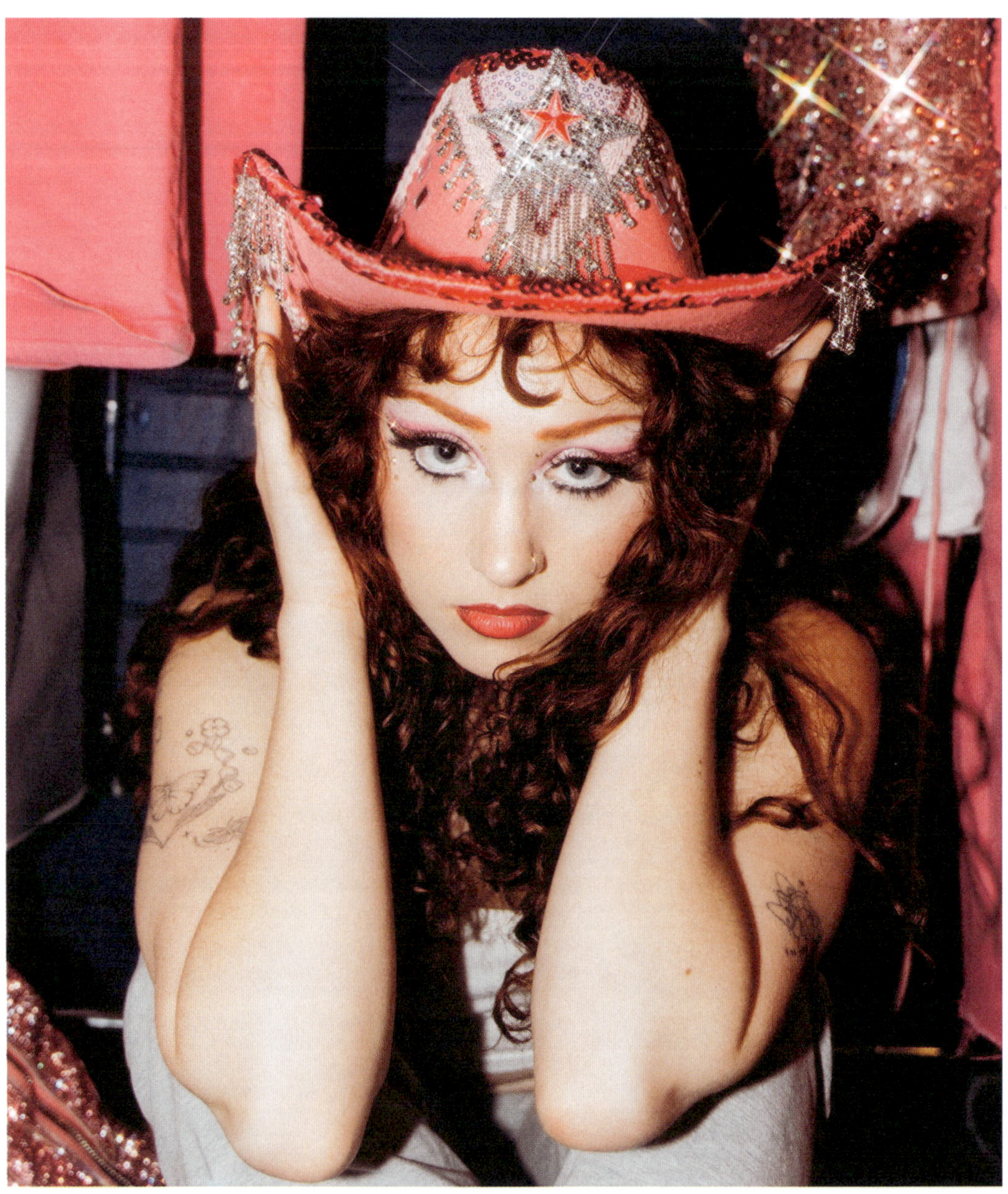

RISE AND FALL OF A MIDWEST PRINCESS

On 22 September 2023, after months of touring, releasing singles and videos, and building the kind of super-dedicated fanbase that many artists can only dream of, Chappell finally released her debut full-length album, *The Rise and Fall of a Midwest Princess*. The record – genre-defying, electrifying and powerful – caught the attention of critics and music fans alike.

'Every song is inspired by something that's real, or something I really longed for. But it's all a very exaggerated, dramatic version of real life,'[43] she told *Polyester*.

Since the album's release, Chappell has also shared that writing it helped her come to terms with her queerness: something she actually started writing about before she'd found herself able to fully express it in real life. She told Grammy.com: 'Music allows me to express anything, even things I've never experienced before. It allows me to express queerness, even if it was only daydreams at that point.'[44]

In an interview with *Nylon*, she shared the story of her first gay kiss, and how liberated she felt in that moment: 'I was crying. It was the first time I'd ever kissed a girl. I was like, "I am queer. I actually am."'[45]

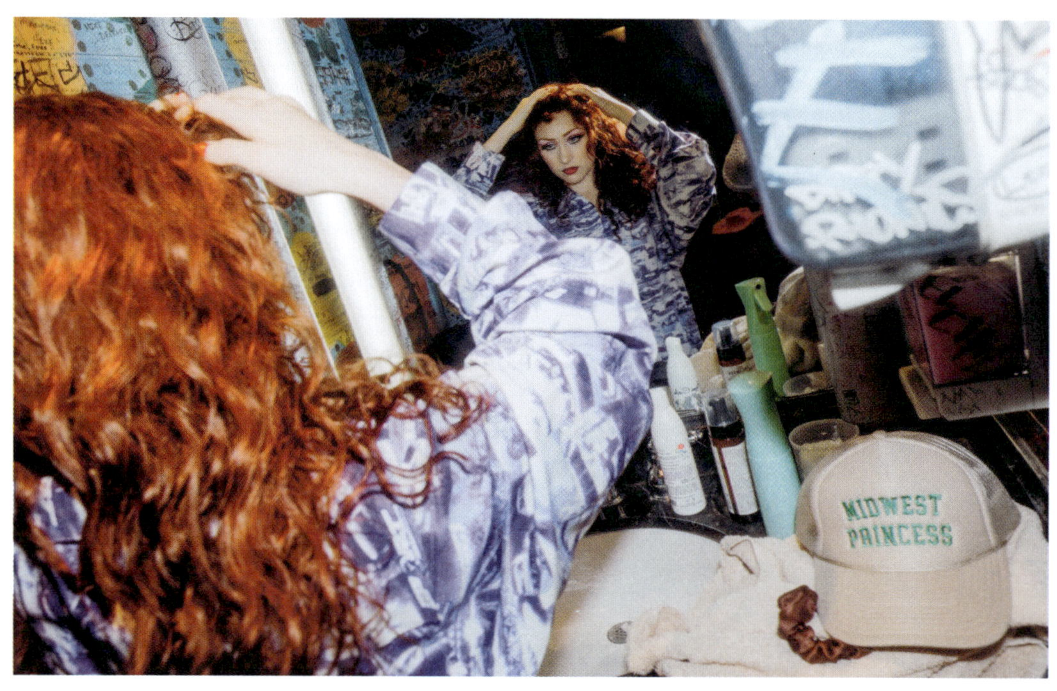
MIDWEST
PRINCESS

MIDWEST PRINCESS ON TOUR

To mark the album's release, Chappell set off on the epic 89-show The Midwest Princess Tour across the US and Canada, followed by shows in Australia, Germany, the Netherlands, France and England – closing out the year at London's iconic gay club, Heaven. Despite the number of dates and the sharp increase in recognition, Chappell kept the shows playful and creative, continuing to involve local drag artists and inviting her audience to dress up. Part of the show also involved her serenading a wig on a mic stand – which admittedly sounds bizarre, but was actually oddly touching.

Meanwhile, accolades for the album were pouring in thick and fast. *The Rise and Fall of a Midwest Princess* was listed as among the best records of 2023 by *Time*, *Rolling Stone*, *Nylon* and *Pitchfork*.

SHE'S OLIVIA'S NUMBER ONE

Towards the end of 2023, pop sensation Olivia Rodrigo shared that her love for Chappell Roan runs deep. In an interview with the *Hollywood Reporter*, Rodrigo said: 'My Spotify Wrapped just came out. I think my number one artist was Chappell Roan. She just put out her first album, and Dan, my producer, produced it, and it's amazing. So I'm listening to a lot of her.'

Rodrigo also asked Chappell to open for her on the US leg of her Guts World Tour in February and March 2024, meaning she was playing huge venues and arenas – for some dates, there were crowds of up to 32,000 fans.

She later told BBC Radio 1: 'I was obsessed with Hannah Montana when I was little,' explaining that her first ever concert was watching Hannah Montana and the Jonas Brothers. Sixteen years later, 'I was just, like, in shock when I opened for Olivia ... that, like, I'd played in the same venue that I saw Hannah Montana in.'[46] During the tour, Chappell joined Rodrigo on stage for a performance of 'HOT TO GO!', much to the delight of fans.

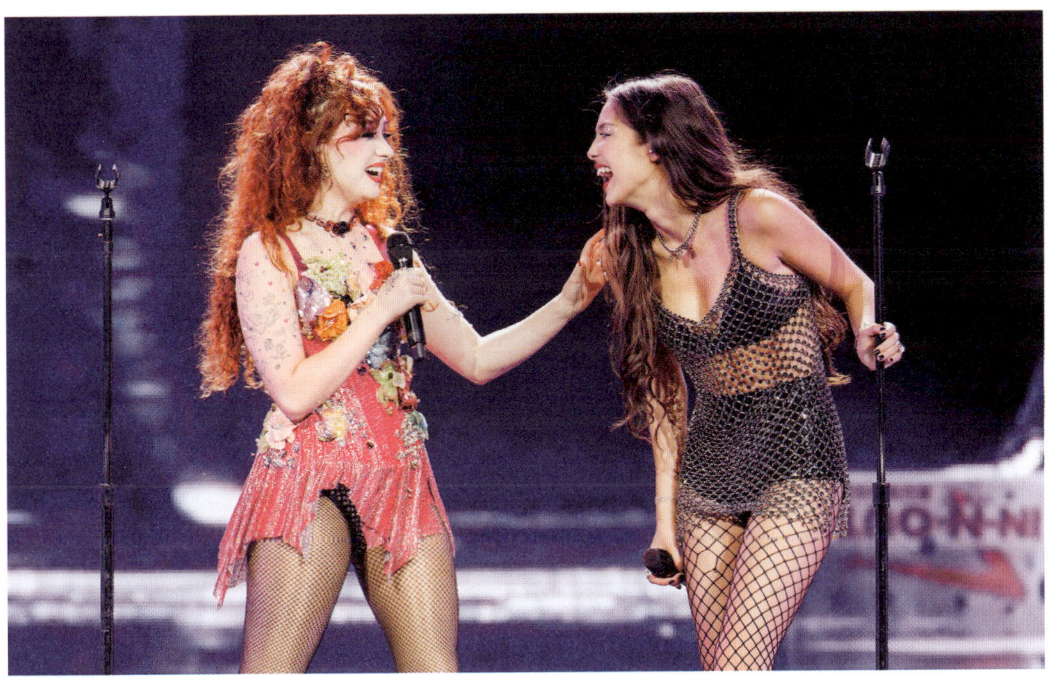

YOUR FAVOURITE ARTIST'S FAVOURITE ARTIST

The highlights pile up thick and fast as her meteoric rise continues.

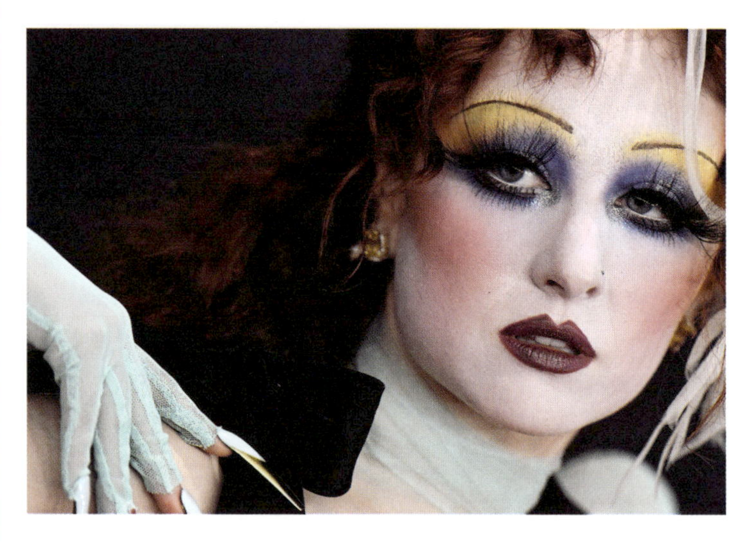

'YOU DO NOT NEED
TO TAKE THIS SERIOUSLY:
IT'S POP MUSIC.'[47]

TINY DESK, HUGE PERSONALITY

In March 2024, Chappell performed a Tiny Desk Concert for the radio station, NPR. Tiny Desk Concerts began in 2008, and feature selected artists performing a live concert at the desk of *All Songs Considered* host Bob Boilen. Over the years, singers from Weird Al Yankovic to Taylor Swift and Harry Styles have graced this iconic desk, but nobody has done it quite like Chappell Roan.

With a set list made up of 'Casual', 'Pink Pony Club', 'Picture You', 'California' and 'Red Wine Supernova', she wowed with stunning vocals and a playful approach, revealing to great cheers between songs, 'I love NPR, guys, I'm serious! Wait – I donate. Yeah … yeah, not to brag. Yeah, like, I'm really giving.'[48] And of course, she brought the look to end all looks: a bright pink gown, with white powdered skin, stunning blue eye make-up, lipstick on her teeth and a towering red wig adorned with butterflies and cigarette butts. Patting this astonishing hairpiece, Chappell revealed that the wig was stuffed with a trash bag – 'That's how we got it so big.'

The organisers were so taken with her crowning glory – and who wouldn't be? – that they asked her to leave it behind as a token of her performance, and it now sits proudly atop a skull donated by Cypress Hill.

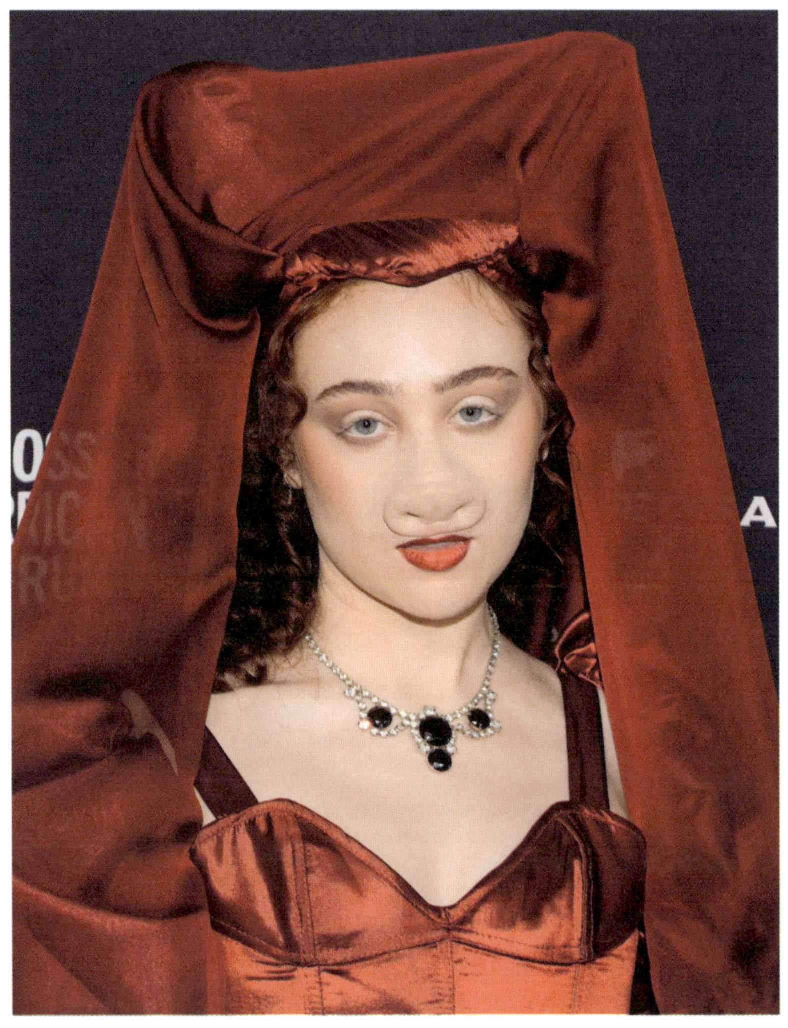

GOOD LUCK, BABE!

On 5 April 2024, Chappell released 'Good Luck, Babe!' – and it soon became clear this would be her breakout song. As Chappell's profile continued to rise over the following months, it became a sleeper hit, ultimately reaching number one in Ireland, number two in the UK and number four in the US.

With a catchy chorus and soaring melodies that show off her impressive vocal range, the song has become a firm favourite with fans, and was accompanied by a lyric video that made gleeful use of cartoonish fonts, bright colours and nineties-style graphics – all very *Clarissa Explains It All*. Other artists were soon inspired to cover the song, with the Jonas Brothers performing their own version during a concert in Florida – a full-circle moment for Chappell, considering they played at the first concert she ever attended (see page 60).

Chappell told BBC Radio 1 that 'Good Luck, Babe!' was 'the first chapter of the new book I'm writing.'[49] We can't wait to read the rest.

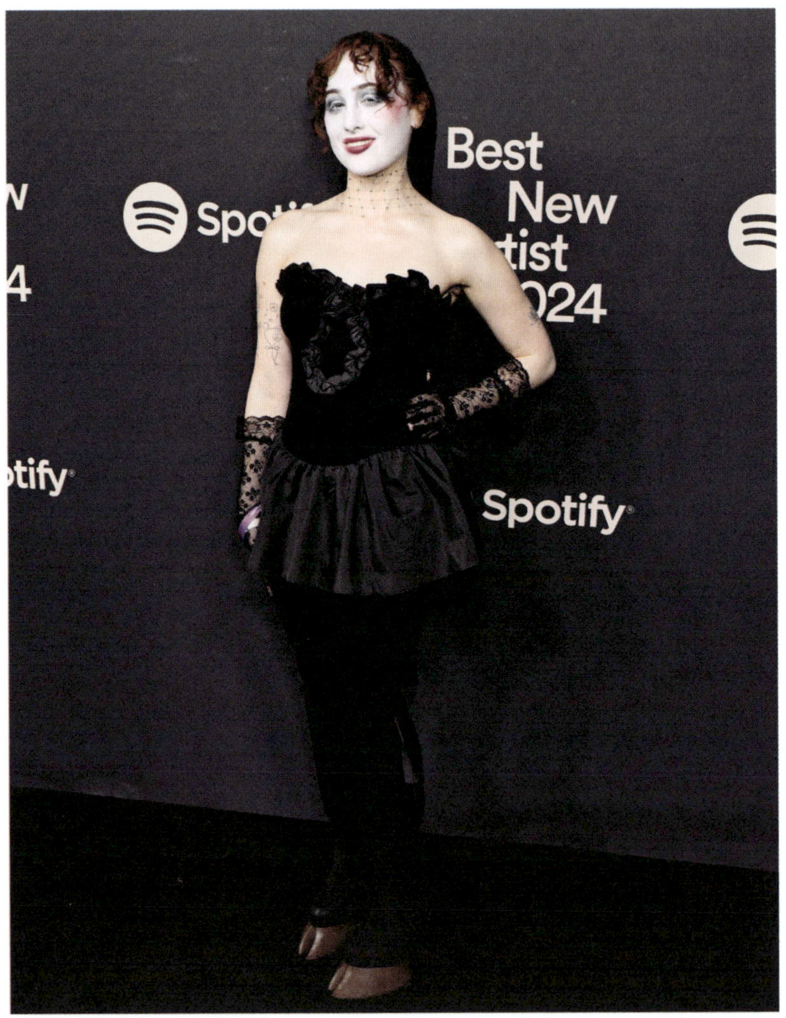
Best
New
Spotify

SLEEPER HITS

'Good Luck, Babe!' wasn't the only sleeper hit for Chappell in 2024. That year, she went from having a few million monthly listeners on Spotify to an incredible 45 million by September. Previous singles started creeping up the charts: 'HOT TO GO!' reached the top ten in the UK, while 'Pink Pony Club' peaked at number two in the UK and number eight in the US, despite having been out for more than four years. To some people, it must have felt as if this fully-fledged pop superstar had just appeared out of nowhere, but the truth is this dizzying success was the result of years of hard work, patience and self-belief.

Reflecting on her success, Chappell told BBC Radio 1: 'It's just really affirming, and really precious, to do performances around the world and have, like, everyone sing [the lyrics] back to you in a country you've never been in. I think that's just so magical.'[50]

THE ROCKET MAN'S SEAL OF APPROVAL

Among Chappell Roan's many celebrity fans is pop legend Elton John – that's right, the Rocket Man himself. She has twice appeared on his podcast *Rocket Hour*: first in September 2023, and again in May 2024. Following their first encounter, Chappell told *Time* that she was so overwhelmed and excited afterwards that she shaved off her eyebrows.[51]

During their second interview, Elton told her: 'For me, as an artist who's been around a long time, seeing you happen [...] has brought me so much joy [...]. I know what you're capable of, and you just make my heart jump when I see you, when I hear you'.[52]

Elton later told *Rolling Stone*: 'I am very protective of her. She is kind, innocent, wonderful. She is not "Chappell Roan" offstage – a bit like me. She is one of those people who I felt like I have known for a long time.'[53]

Since then, the pair of icons have performed duets, with Elton donning a pink cowboy hat for 'Pink Pony Club' when they sang it together at his Oscars party in March 2025.

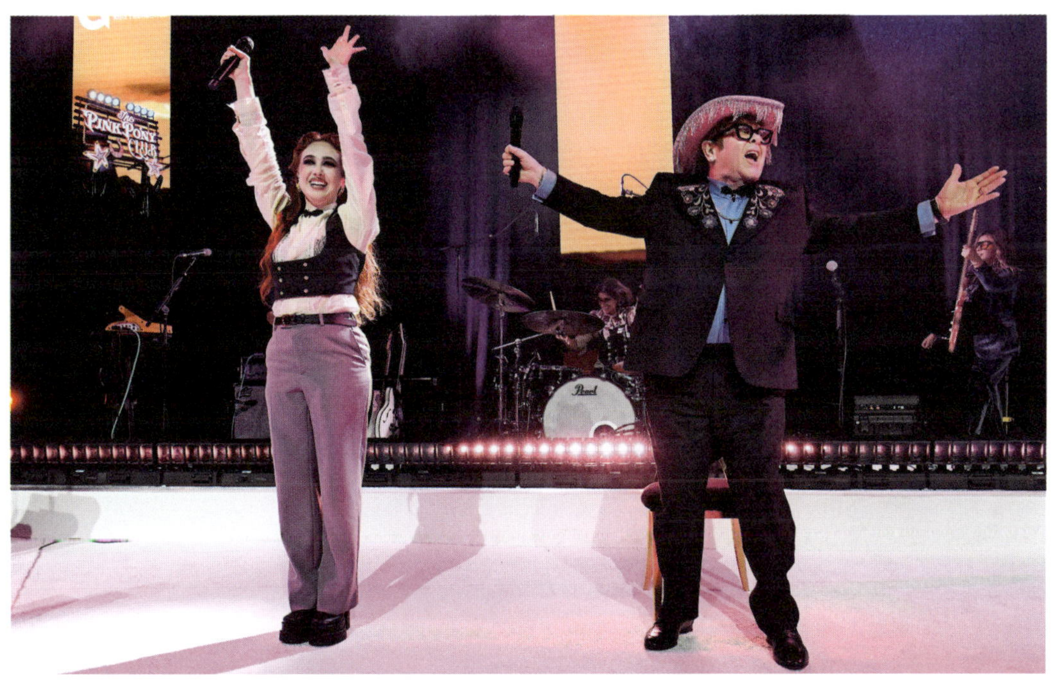
The
PINK PONY
CLUB
Pearl

THE QUEEN OF COACHELLA

In April 2024, Chappell performed at both weekends of the world-renowned festival Coachella, performing on the Gobi Stage. It wasn't just her first time playing this festival – it was her first time playing any festival. In an interview with *Vogue*, she revealed: 'To be playing Coachella as my first festival is surreal. I can't believe it.'[54]

For the first show, she wore a body suit emblazoned with the legend 'Eat Me' and delighted crowds with a high-energy set. When she returned the following weekend, she wore a mesmerising butterfly outfit, complete with enormous wings, and introduced herself as follows: 'My name is Chappell Roan. I'm your favourite artist's favourite artist. I'm your dream girl's dream girl.'

Later, she revealed that this was a reference to drag star Sasha Colby, who has referred to herself as: 'Your favourite drag queen's favourite drag queen'.

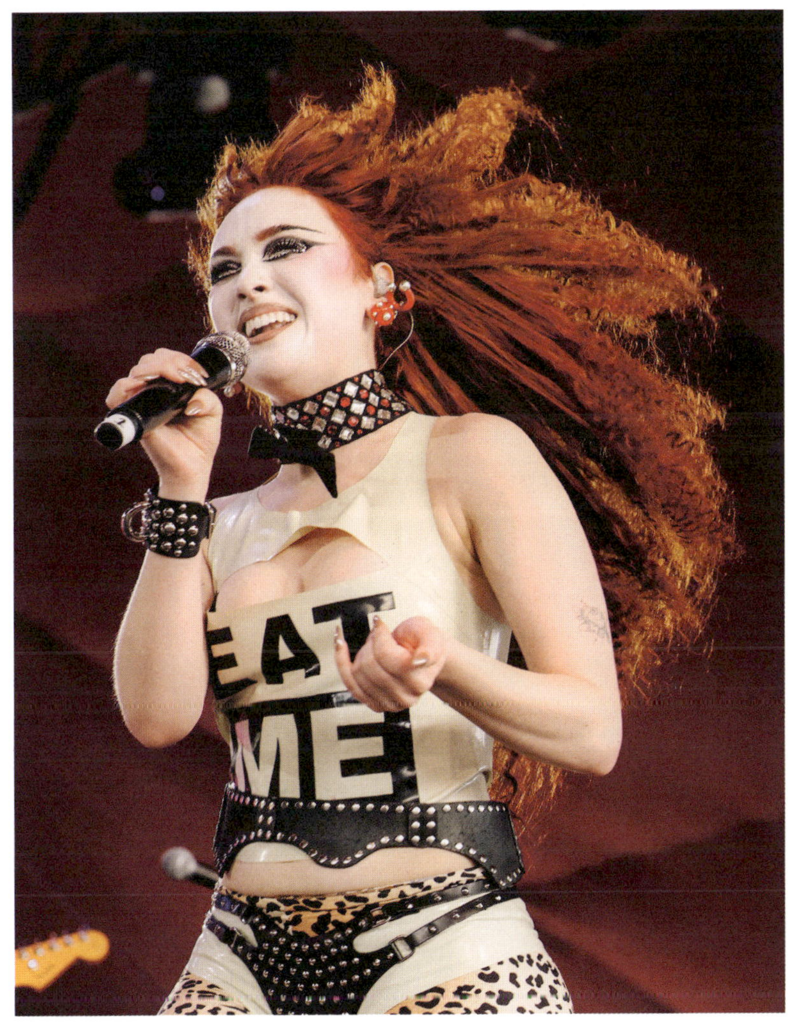
EAT
ME

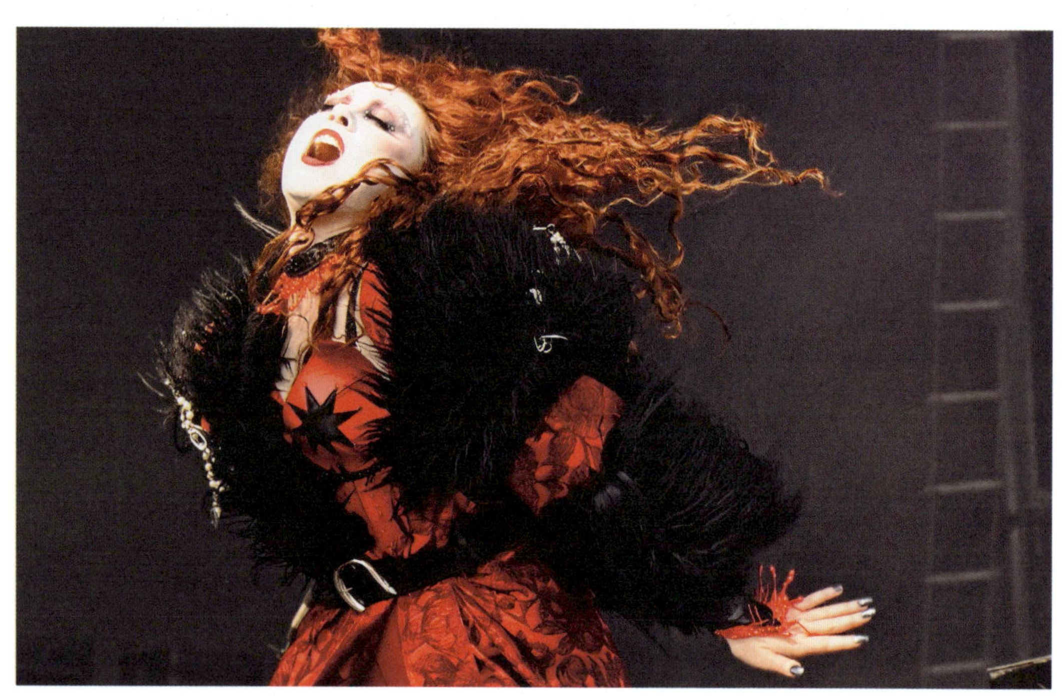

BOSTON CALLED, CHAPPELL ANSWERED

In May 2024, Chappell performed at Boston Calling to a vast crowd of 40,000, many of whom donned pink cowboy hats in anticipation of her set. After her opening track – 'Femininomenon' – she took off her red coat to reveal a red-and-black tasselled leotard with a matching collar. Her trademark red curls hung loose, while her face was painted white, with bold red lips and shimmering eyeshadow.

Dizzying drone footage posted online shows the spectators stretching out into the far distance as she performs 'Red Wine Supernova', while other videos show the hordes of onlookers dancing along with the choreography for 'HOT TO GO!'.

In an Instagram post after the show, Chappell wrote: 'the biggest crowd I've literally ever seen in person. I love festivals [...] oh my god thank u thank u.'[55]

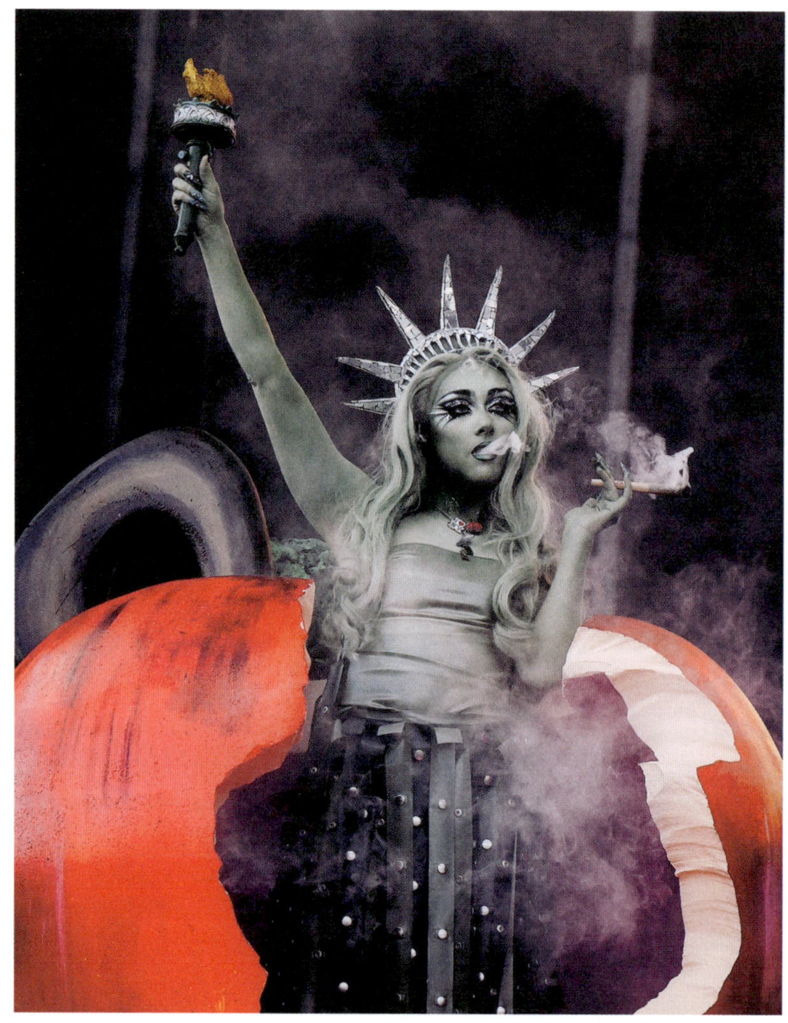

NEW YORK'S GOV BALL

As festival season continued, June 2024 saw Chappell perform at the Governors Ball in New York. It was another mind-bogglingly huge crowd, with fans spilling across the festival site as they tried to get within view of the main stage. For her entrance, she emerged from within an enormous red apple (because New York's the Big Apple, geddit?) and wowed the crowd with her incredible ensemble. Painted green from head to toe, with green hair, a spiked headdress and a torch held aloft, Chappell had shown up dressed as Lady Liberty – and her fans went wild for it. Her band, meanwhile, wore yellow with black-and-white chequered trims, a nod to the city's iconic yellow taxis. Her outfit wasn't the only statement made that day, as we'll see on page 106.

THE TONIGHT SHOW STARRING CHAPPELL ROAN

Later in June 2024, Chappell appeared on *The Tonight Show Starring Jimmy Fallon*, wearing an outfit that featured black feathers, sharp talons and bright blond curls. Jimmy Fallon started the interview by showing Chappell a photograph of her younger self on stage, wearing a simple red jumpsuit and standing behind a keyboard. As they discussed how much things had changed, Chappell talked about her stylist Genesis Webb, and the inspiration behind her iconic onstage looks.

She also showed some of her trademark cheeky humour when she teased Jimmy after he revealed he'd googled her ahead of their meeting, saying: 'Did you not know who I was before?'. Then, when Jimmy revealed that searching for her name caused Google to ask: 'Did you mean your favourite artist's favourite artist?', referencing her Coachella performance (see page 72), she declared: 'I didn't do that [...] It's this random twink that works at Google. I know it is. I know it's just some assistant that [was] like ... "We love her."'[56]

After the interview, Chappell swapped her obsidian plumes for fluffy white feathers and performed 'Good Luck, Babe!' to rapturous applause from the studio audience.

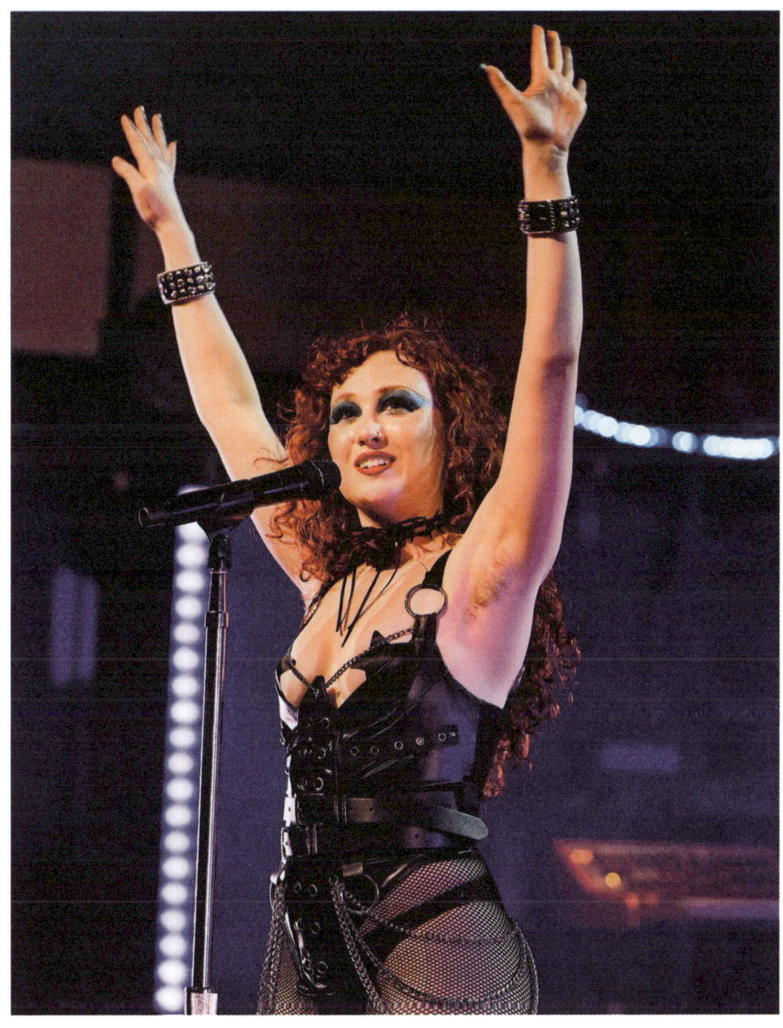

CHAPPELL-PALOOZA

August 2024 saw Chappell's run of festival performances continue with Lollapalooza – and another unbelievably vast crowd. A festival spokesperson told CNN: 'Chappell's performance was the biggest daytime set we've ever seen,' while other sources speculated that it was the biggest crowd the festival had ever drawn full stop.[57] The *LA Times* reported that Chappell had originally been scheduled to play a smaller stage, but as her fandom rapidly grew in the lead-up to the festival, the organisers hastily swapped things around so that she could perform on the main stage – and it's lucky they did.[58]

Chappell stepped out onstage dressed in a stunning pink-and-blue wrestler's outfit, complete with mask. The band wore matching outfits and the drumkit was elevated in its very own wrestling ring.

After a set that thrilled the many thousands watching, Chappell posted on Instagram: 'I was crying as I walked onstage at @lollapalooza because of the overwhelm of support. Thank you thank you thank you. I will remember this forever.'[59]

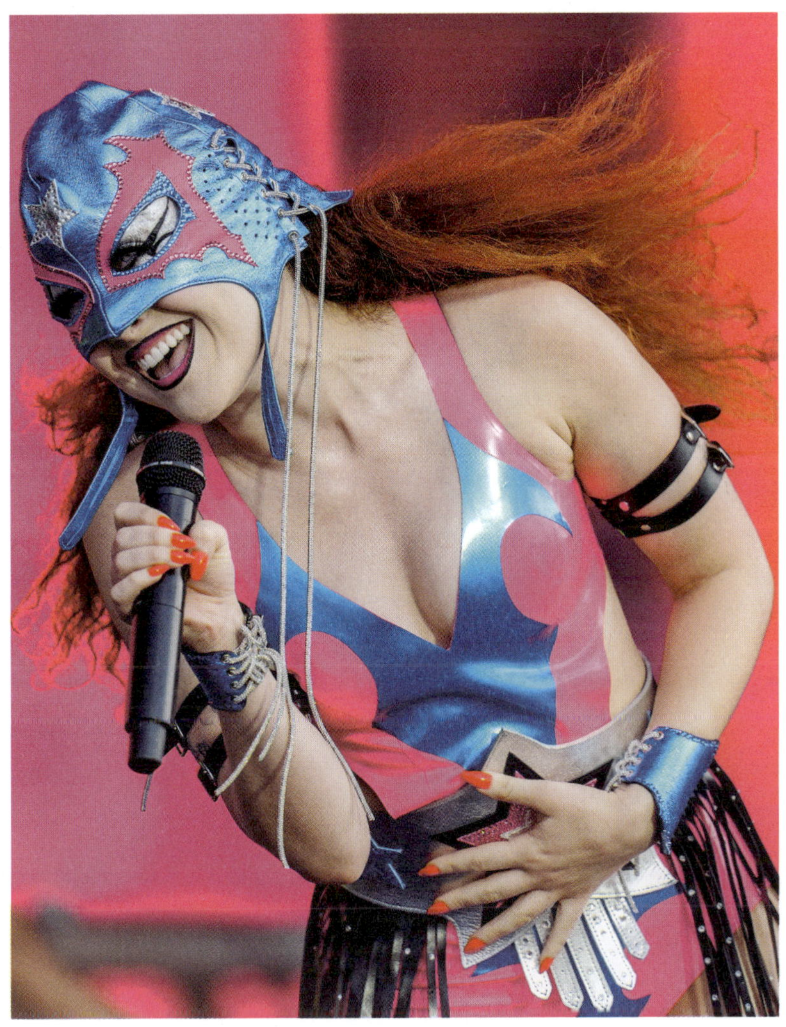

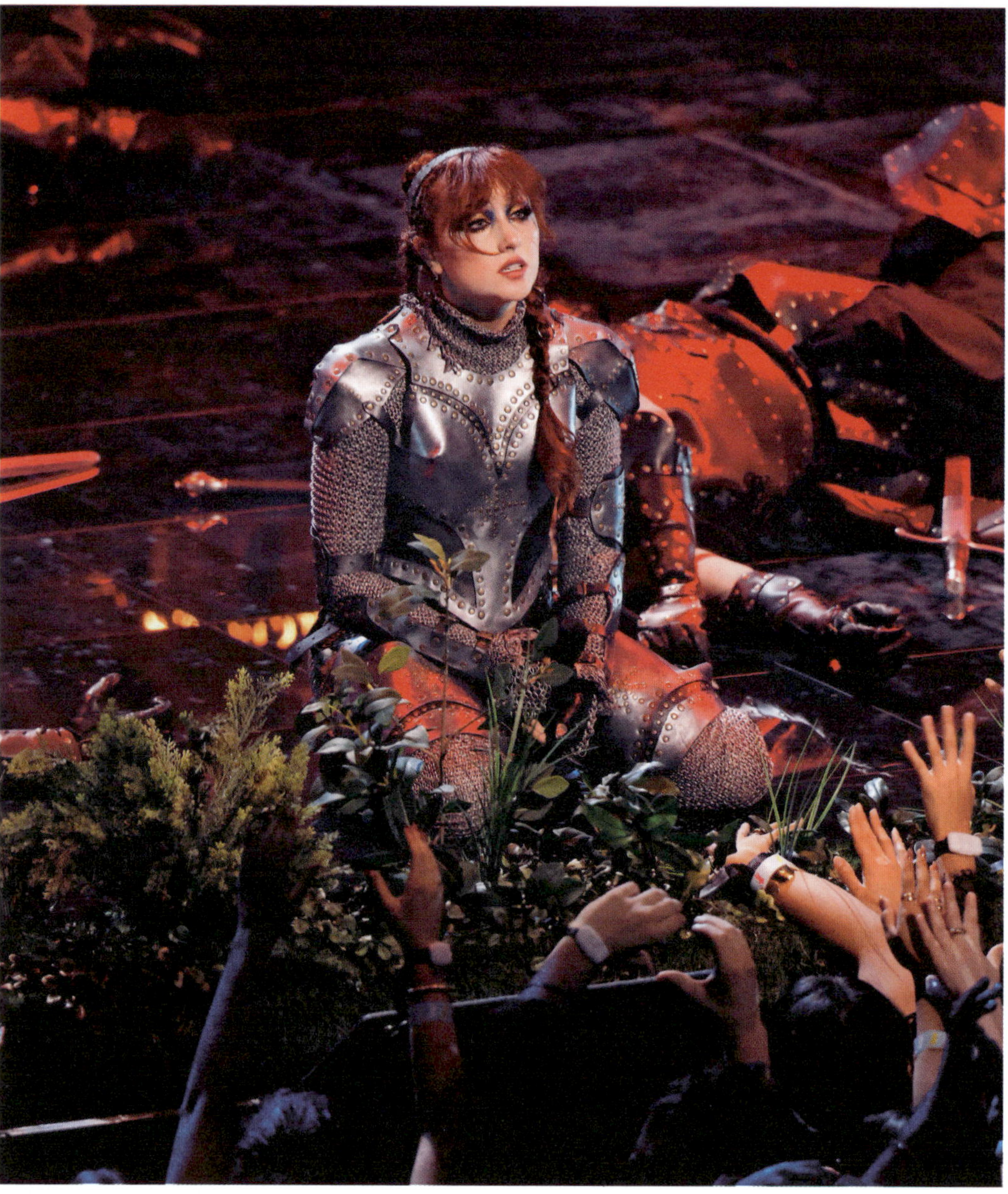

SIR CHAPPELL

In September 2024, Chappell attended the VMAs – in full medieval regalia. For her red carpet walk (which was not without incident – see page 98), she wore a sheer gown, topped with a pale green velvet robe, with metal talons for nails and a full-length sword.

The theme continued through several costume changes. She performed 'Good Luck, Babe!' during the show, dressed in a full suit of armour and brandishing a crossbow from which she shot a flaming arrow, setting the castle-themed set ablaze as she sang. Later, she told the *Guardian* '"Good Luck, Babe!" doesn't warrant me coming out with a weapon on fire, but I was like, I have to do it. This is what I really would have wanted as my eleven-year-old-boy version of myself.'[60]

That night, Chappell won the Best New Artist award – and accepted it in yet another medieval outfit, this time a stunning hooded gown made of chainmail.

One of the many highlights of the evening was the moment that drag legend Sasha Colby introduced Chappell to the stage. You'll remember that Chappell paraphrased Sasha during her epic Coachella performance (see page 72): well, that moment came full circle when Sasha announced: 'The Midwest Princess is in the house. Your favourite drag queen's favourite artist: here is my daughter, Chappell Roan!'[61]

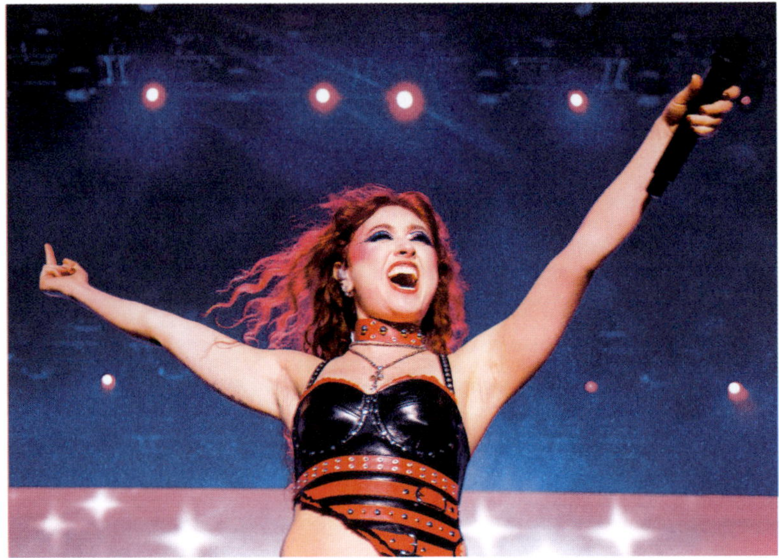

THE CONTINUED RISE OF A MIDWEST PRINCESS

With the buzz around Chappell Roan reaching deafening levels, *The Rise and Fall of a Midwest Princess* continued to climb the charts, peaking at number two on the US Billboard charts and reaching number one in the UK, Ireland and New Zealand, while also hitting number three in Australia.

In an interview, Chappell told BBC Radio 1: 'I've never been worried about gaining a fanbase, because it's just something you can't force.'[62]

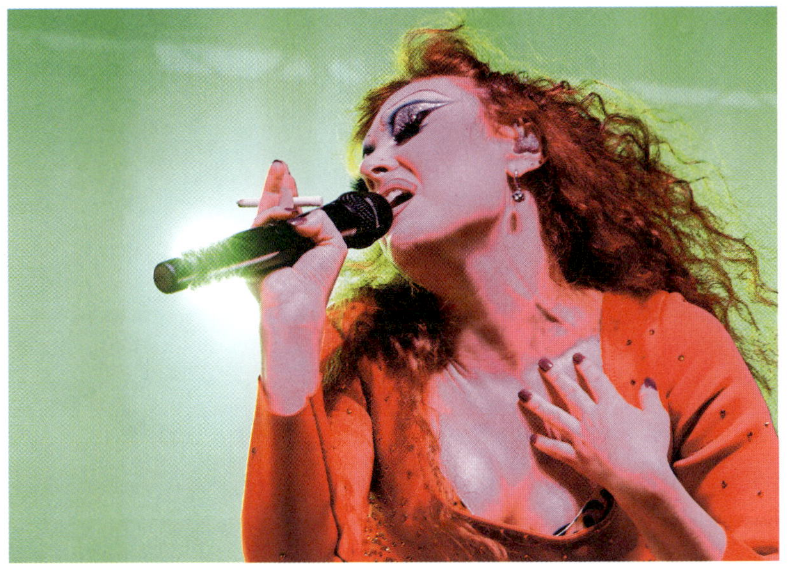

SATURDAY NIGHT LIVE, BABY

November 2024 saw Chappell appear as the musical guest on *Saturday Night Live*. The day before the show aired, she shared an old Facebook post with her fans, dated 23 April 2011, in which one Kayleigh Amstutz wrote: 'I am determined to be on SNL.' She made it.

Chappell performed 'Pink Pony Club' while wearing a shimmering pale gown, with her hair teased into huge curls adorned with Lily Munster-esque white streaks. Later, she changed into pale pink gingham hotpants and cowboy boots to perform a new country-style song called 'The Giver'.

MAKE THE WINS GO ON AND ON

In January 2025, Chappell was voted winner of BBC Radio 1's annual poll and named their Sound of 2025. Previous winners include Adele (2008), Ellie Goulding (2010) and Sam Smith (2014), and the judges were made up of industry experts, music critics and fellow artists, including Dua Lipa and Elton John (whose love for Chappell is no secret, as we have seen).

Her success continued in February, when she won the Grammy Award for Best New Artist, an accolade that has previously gone to icons including Olivia Rodrigo, Billie Eilish and Dua Lipa. Chappell was also nominated in several other categories, including Song of the Year and Album of the Year.

During the awards ceremony, she gave yet another dazzling performance of 'Pink Pony Club'. The audience must have known they were in for a treat when the lights came up to reveal Chappell astride a giant pink pony in the middle of the stage. She wore a feathered, glittering Stetson and was backed up by an entire troupe of cowboy dancers wearing clown face paint. The performance was met with rapturous applause from the crowd of celebrity attendees, including John Legend and Cynthia Erivo.

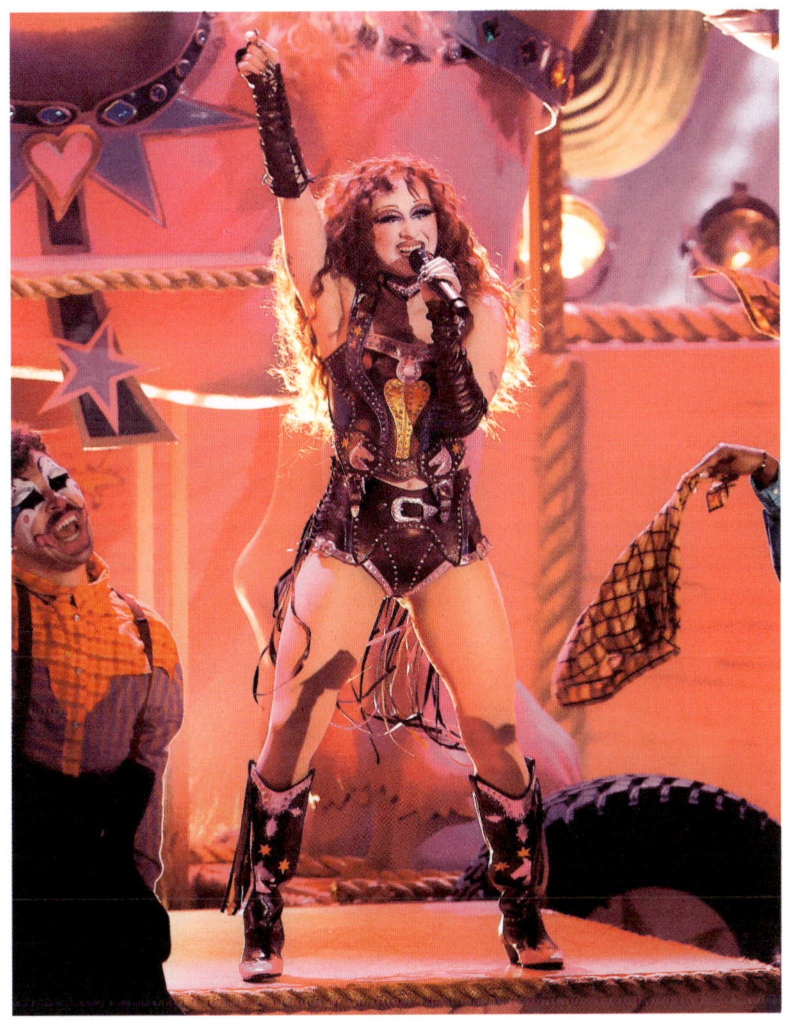

QUEEN OF THE BRITS

In March 2025, Chappell won two Brit Awards: International Song of the Year for 'Good Luck, Babe!', and International Artist of the Year, beating competition from an incredible list of nominees including Beyoncé, Kendrick Lamar, Billie Eilish and Taylor Swift. Although she was unable to attend in person, Chappell appeared via video link to accept her awards.

Danny Dyer, who presented the award for International Song of the Year, should probably check out our tutorial on how to pronounce her name (see page 25): it's not 'Chappell Row-en', Danny! In her acceptance speech for the award, Chappell said: 'Over the years, I have written many songs. I don't believe in bad art, but let's just say I had to write a lot of bad songs to get to the good ones.'[63]

Luckily, Vicky McClure, presenting International Artist of the Year, knew how to say Chappell's name – and the queen of the hour responded by putting on her best English accent and saying: 'It's so lit that I'm winning a Brit.'[64]

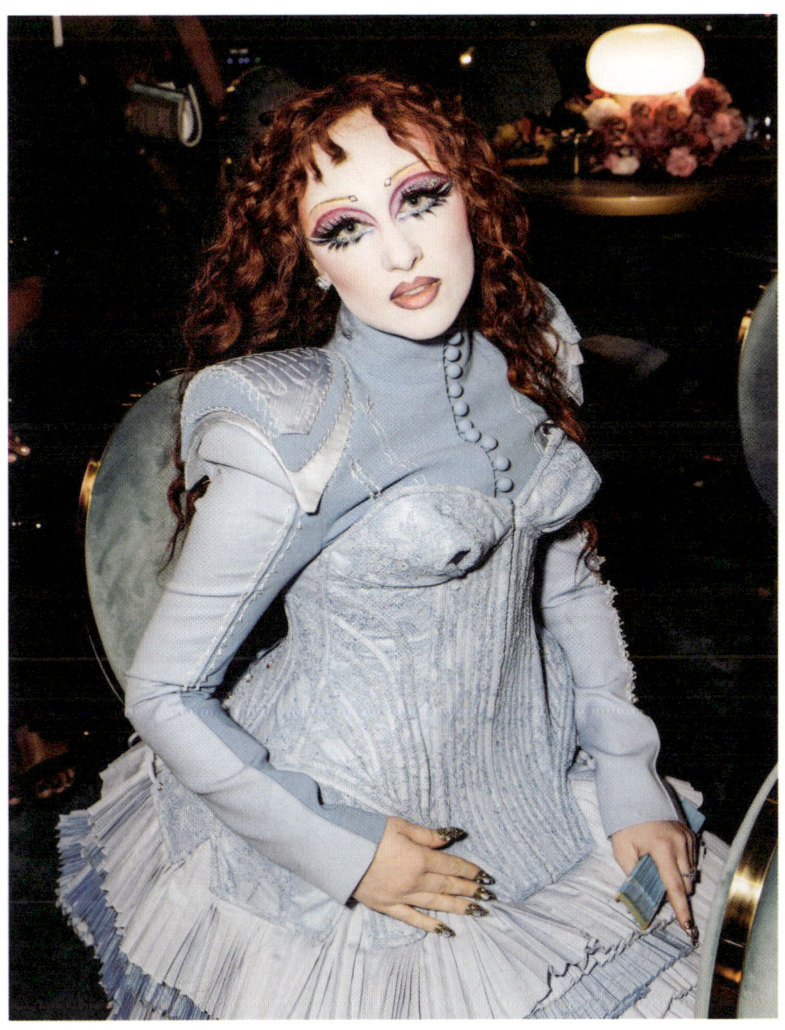

BOLD, BRAVE, ICONIC

Chappell is known for her playful and witty repartee between songs on tour, during interviews and online, and also for being open and honest in a way that is deeply refreshing. Here are some of her funniest, bravest and most vulnerable moments.

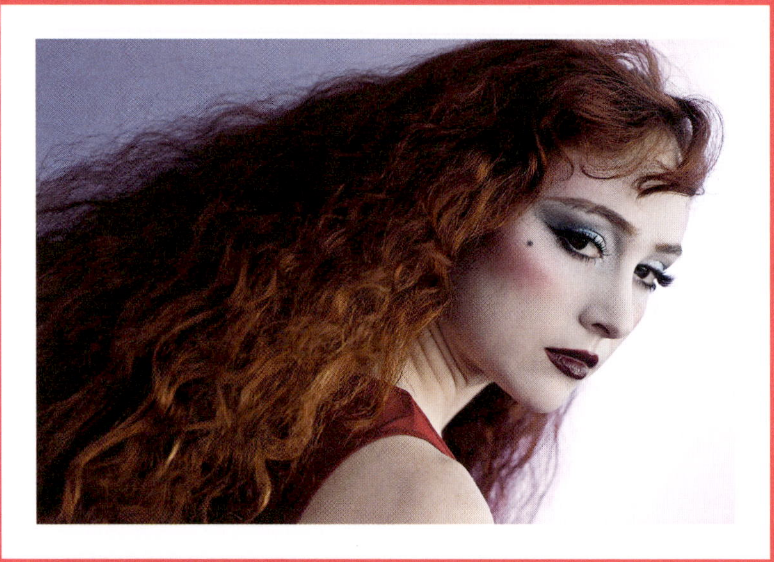

'NO ONE PERFORMS BETTER THAN A DRAG QUEEN.'[65]

SAOIRSE ROAN

When she isn't wearing white foundation, bejewelled eyebrows and dustings of colourful eyeshadow, fans have often said how much a barefaced Chappell Roan looks like Hollywood star Saoirse Ronan. So many people pointed it out that Chappell responded by posting a TikTok video showing an image of Saoirse morphing into her, captioned: 'Holy fuck remember when I was in the lovely bones?'[66]

Years later, Saoirse Ronan appeared on *The Tonight Show Starring Jimmy Fallon* and revealed that she was aware of the comparison – because Chappell had told her about it herself.

'I became so obsessed with her over the summer, just like everyone else,' Saoirse explained. '[…] She's just incredible.' So Saoirse went along to one of Chappell's shows, along with Brie Larson, naturally) and afterwards they introduced themselves. Saoirse said she was trying to play it cool, but Chappell called her over and said, 'Oh, everyone says that we're the same.'

Just to prove that they're *not* the same person, Chappell and Saoirse even snapped a photo.

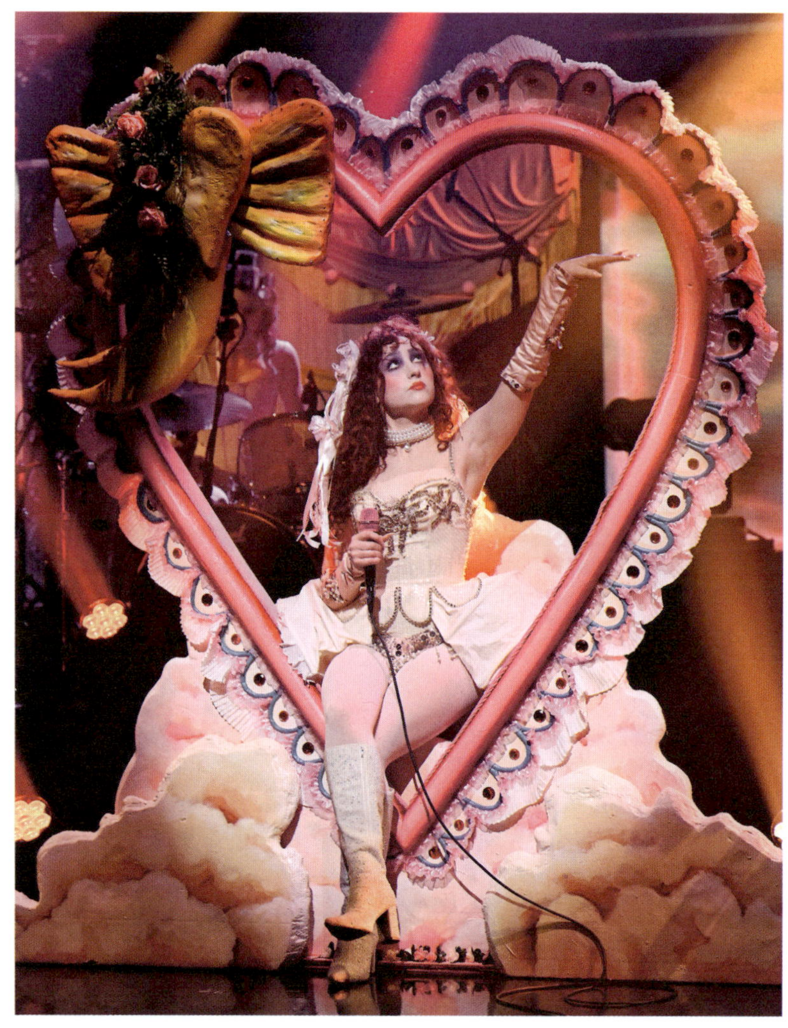

IT'S A DRAG

'A drag queen does not get on stage to calm people down. A drag queen does not say things to flatter people. A queen makes you blush, you know what I mean? Expect the same energy at my show.' [67]

Chappell has often talked about how much her onstage style is inspired by drag culture, with 'Chappell Roan' essentially being her drag persona. In an interview with *Vanity Fair*, she explained: 'Being a queen is just like – you're in make-up and hair and you exude all your energy and you're very dramatic.'[68]

She later told BBC Radio 1: '[Drag queens] push me to go bigger with my outfits, go bolder with my lyrics, just really let go when it comes to performing on stage ... Drag queens [and burlesque dancers] are my biggest inspiration – just any kind of that really hypnotising, outrageous spectacle.'[69]

As well as booking local drag artists as her supporting acts whenever she's on tour, Chappell has been extremely vocal about how important it is to her to create a safe space at her shows for people to dress and express themselves as they wish. She encourages her fans to join her in dressing up and celebrating extravagant outfits, and posts dress-up themes for her concerts about a month ahead of time so fans have the opportunity to put together their outfits.

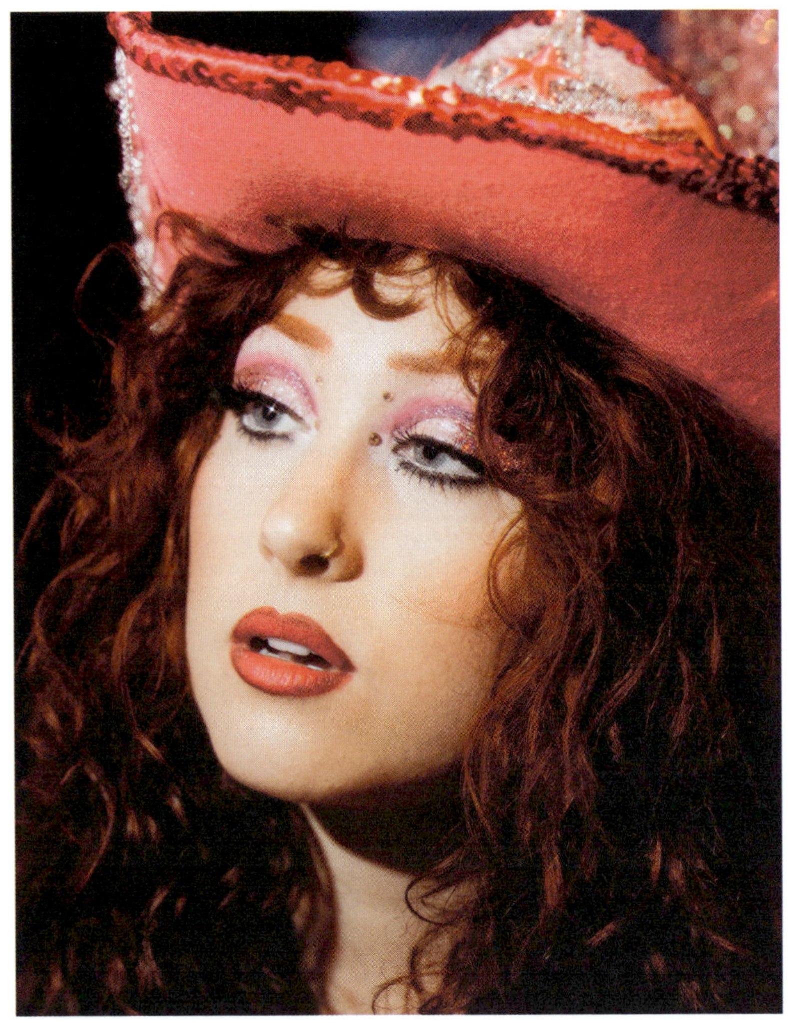

MENTAL HEALTH AND BEING REAL

In 2022, Chappell shared her bipolar diagnosis with fans, encouraging open and empathetic conversations about mental health. She later told *Vanity Fair*: 'Bipolar disorder is one of the hardest to treat because you just don't know what's gonna make you feel better. I mean, it took me two years [after diagnosis] to find the right medications and, holy cow, it was so hard!'[70]

She has also spoken openly and honestly about how hard it was to grow up with an undiagnosed condition. In an interview with *The Face*, she explained: 'All I want in life is to feel like a good person, because I felt like such a bad person my whole life – the worst kid in the family, always so out of control and angry … It's been really hard to forgive […] myself [and say] dude, you were unmedicated, going through puberty, and refused to believe you were anxious or depressed.'[71]

SHOUTING BACK

The 2024 VMAs was a night of triumph for Chappell, from her Best New Artist win to her stunning performance (see page 83), but it wasn't all plain sailing.

As she made her way into the event, she was faced with a rude photographer who shouted at her to 'shut the fuck up' on the red carpet. But our Chappell is no shrinking violet, and she gave as good as she got, confronting the man who had shouted by raising one of those stunning metal talons and saying, 'No, *you* shut the fuck up.'

Some people criticised her for answering back, but most praised her for standing up for herself. Later, she told the *Guardian*: 'I'm not gonna be a sweetie pie to a man who's telling me to shut the fuck up.'[72] In another interview, she explained: 'I was looking around, and I was like, "This is what people are OK with all the time? And I'm supposed to act normal? This is not normal. This is crazy."'[73]

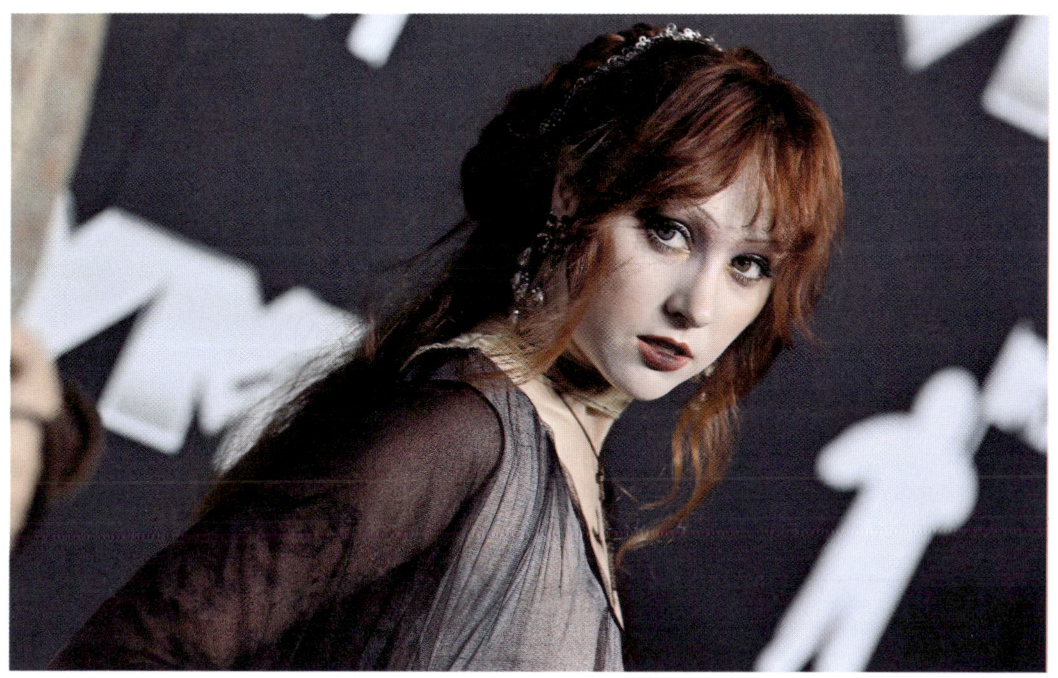

NOBODY IS TOO COOL FOR 'HOT TO GO!'

During her electrifying live sets, Chappell has taken to teaching the crowd the choreography to her hit 'HOT TO GO!', so they can dance along with her by using their arms to spell out the letters H-O-T-T-O-G-O. It's typically a fan-favourite moment, and TikTok is awash with videos of Chapellites performing the iconic moves. Reflecting on the importance of audience participation, Chappell said in one interview: 'I've never really liked concerts where you attend and it feels like you're just standing in the audience, watching someone … I wanted my audience to feel like they're in on it with me.'[74]

However, during her performance at San Francisco's Outside Lands festival in August 2024, Chappell noticed that not everyone in the 50,000-strong crowd was joining in.[75] As she skipped across the stage in the blue sequinned body suit she also wears in the song's video, she cried out: 'It's so weird that VIP thinks they're so way too cool to do this!' before turning to the offending VIPs and screaming 'You're not fuuuuuuuun! Be fun and try!'

If Chappell Roan tells you to dance, you dance.

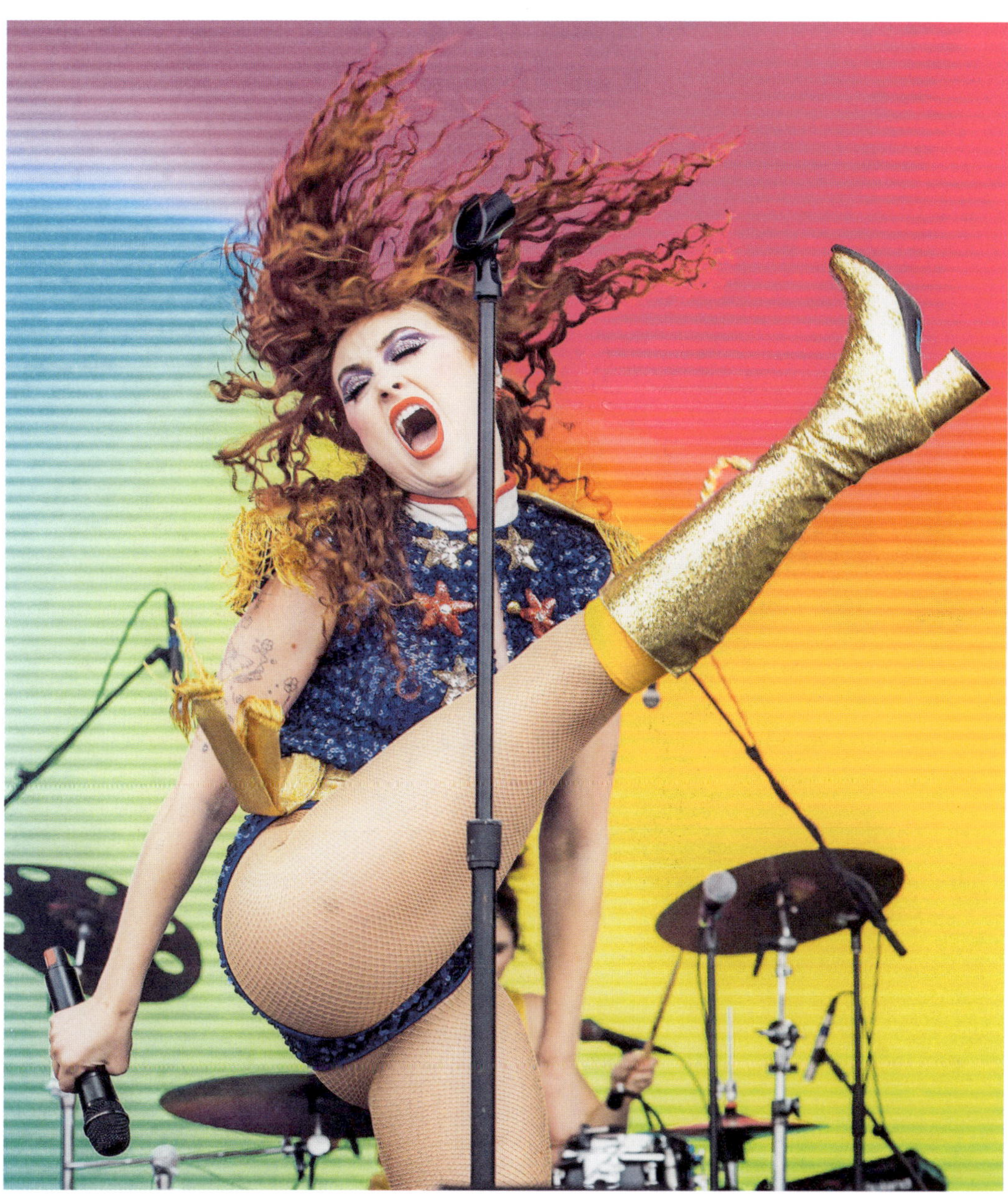

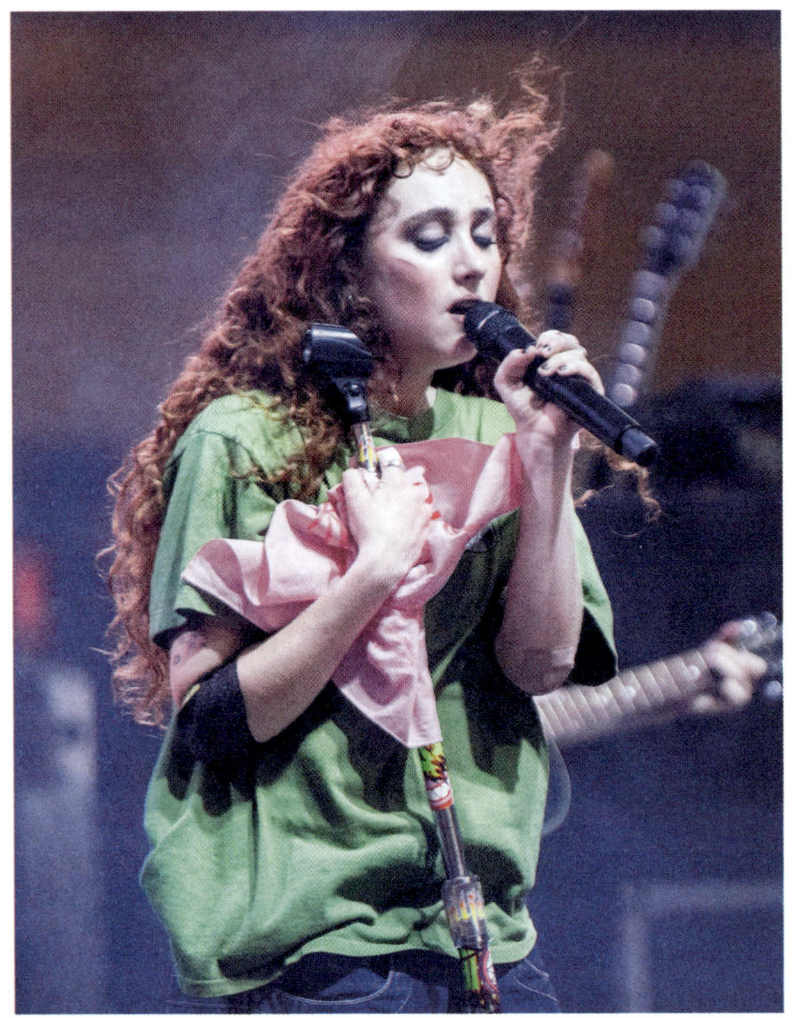

THE CHALLENGES OF FAME

Chappell has been refreshingly open about the unique challenges of fame and the pressures faced by artists in the music industry, winning praise from other celebrities and artists for her honesty and bravery in speaking out. In an interview with *The Face*, she laid it out: 'This industry and artistry thrive on mental illness, burnout, overworking yourself, overextending yourself, not sleeping. You get bigger the more unhealthy you are. Isn't that so fucked up?'[76]

In June 2024, Chappell admitted during a concert that she was feeling overwhelmed by her rapid and meteoric rise to fame. Addressing the crowd, she said: 'I just feel a little off today. I think that my career's just kind of gone really fast, and it's really hard to keep up. [...] I'm just being honest that I'm having a hard time today. So I'm sorry [...] I'm not trying to give you a lesser show. It's just there's a lot going on.'[77]

Fans responded with cheers and love, with many praising her for being real about what she's facing.

Reflecting on that moment with *Rolling Stone*, Chappell explained: 'I was trying so hard to do the theatre-kid thing and just be, like, "Push through! Be the character!" ... I was worried [about] letting people down I wasn't serving that day, and I had to be honest.'[78]

Speaking to the *Guardian*, she shared how overwhelming the changes to her world have been: '[My] whole life has changed ... Everything that I really love to do now comes with baggage. If I want to go thrifting, I have to book security and prepare myself that this is not going to be normal.'[79]

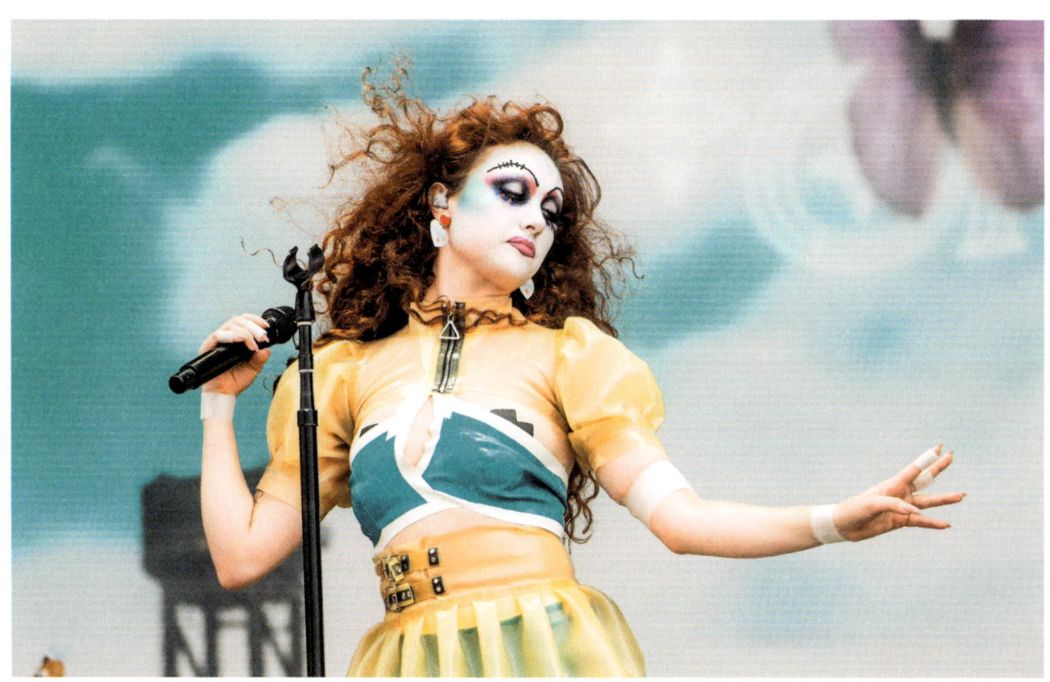

IF YOU WANT TO SEE A CLOWN ...

One of Chappell's signature looks is the iconic super-pale or white foundation she so often sports onstage – but there's more to it than just the way it looks.

'I love a pure white face,' she told drag queen Trixie Mattel. 'I started to do that because that's what the country boys called gay people in my hometown. Clowns ... I was like, "Bitch, I'll show you a clown, if you want to see a clown."'[80]

Eagle-eyed fans will spot the theme of clowns appearing again and again in Chappell's videos, outfits and live performances: there's her white heart-shaped face paint (and clown-faced ex) in the video for 'My Kink is Karma', and of course the dozens of cowboy clowns who joined her onstage at the Grammys. Her cowboy hat even had a little clown design on it. By repeatedly playing with this clown motif, Chappell has reclaimed her power and identity in the most iconic way possible.

REJECTING THE WHITE HOUSE

During that now-legendary set at the Governors Ball in June 2024 (see page 77), Chappell had some strong words to share. As she stood before the vast crowd dressed in her stunning Lady Liberty outfit, she said: 'Today I am in drag as the biggest queen of all – but in case you have forgotten what's etched on my toes …' She looked across the audience, then began to recite the words that are inscribed across the base of the Statue of Liberty, which come from a poem by Emma Lazarus: 'Give me your tired, your poor, / Your huddled masses yearning to breathe free, / The wretched refuse of your teeming shore.'

As the crowd roared their approval, Chappell went on: 'That means freedom and trans rights. That means freedom and women's rights. And […] it especially means freedom for all oppressed people in occupied territories.'[81]

Later in the set, Chappell also revealed that she had turned down an invitation to perform at the White House for Pride. 'We want liberty, justice and freedom for all. When you do that, that's when I'll come.'[82]

And then she burst into a rousing rendition of 'My Kink is Karma'. The queen had well and truly spoken.

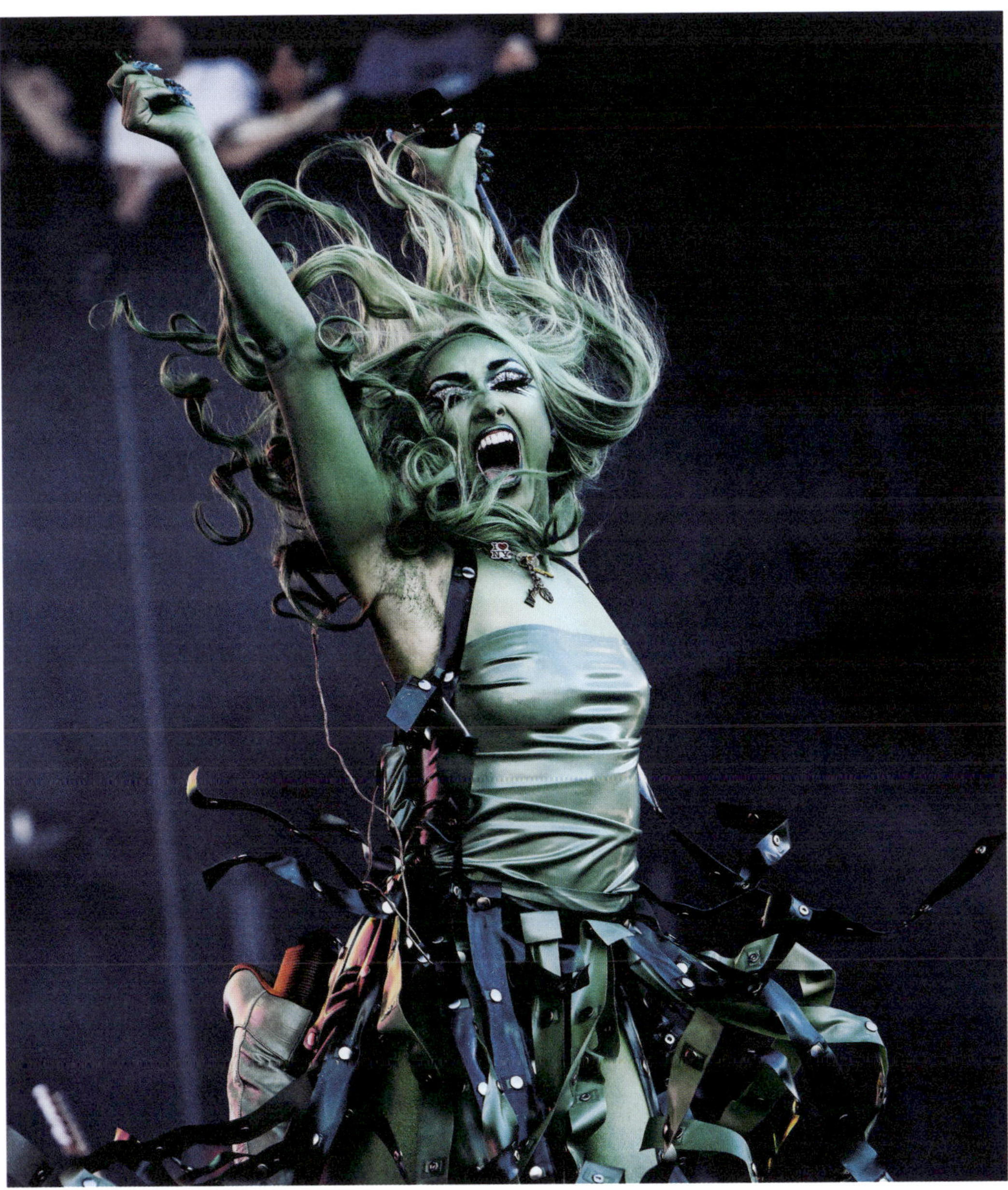

SPEAKING OUT AND SPEAKING UP

When she stepped up to accept her Best New Artist Grammy – wearing a long princess-style conical hat (which did fall off mid-speech) and a ruffled short dress with a long train, Chappell was determined to use her moment for what mattered most. After her list of heartfelt thank yous, she launched into a powerful speech about the music industry, calling on record labels and the powers that be to do better for their artists.

With her voice slightly shaking, she said: 'I told myself if I ever won a Grammy, and I got to stand up here in front of the most powerful people in music, I would demand that labels and the industry profiting millions of dollars off of artists would offer a liveable wage and healthcare, especially to developing artists.'[83]

As the crowd responded with resounding applause, she reflected on how hard it had been for her when she was signed and then dropped at a young age, with very little support from the industry: 'It was so devastating to feel so committed to my art and feel so betrayed by the system [...] If my label [had] prioritised artists' health, I could have been provided care by a company I was giving everything to.'

She finished by looking straight into the camera and saying 'Labels: we got you – but do you got us?'

Her speech was met with a standing ovation from artists including Taylor Swift and Benson Boone. Once again, Chappell had shown that she is a force to be reckoned with. She may have started out as a Midwest Princess, but she's a queen in the world of music now.

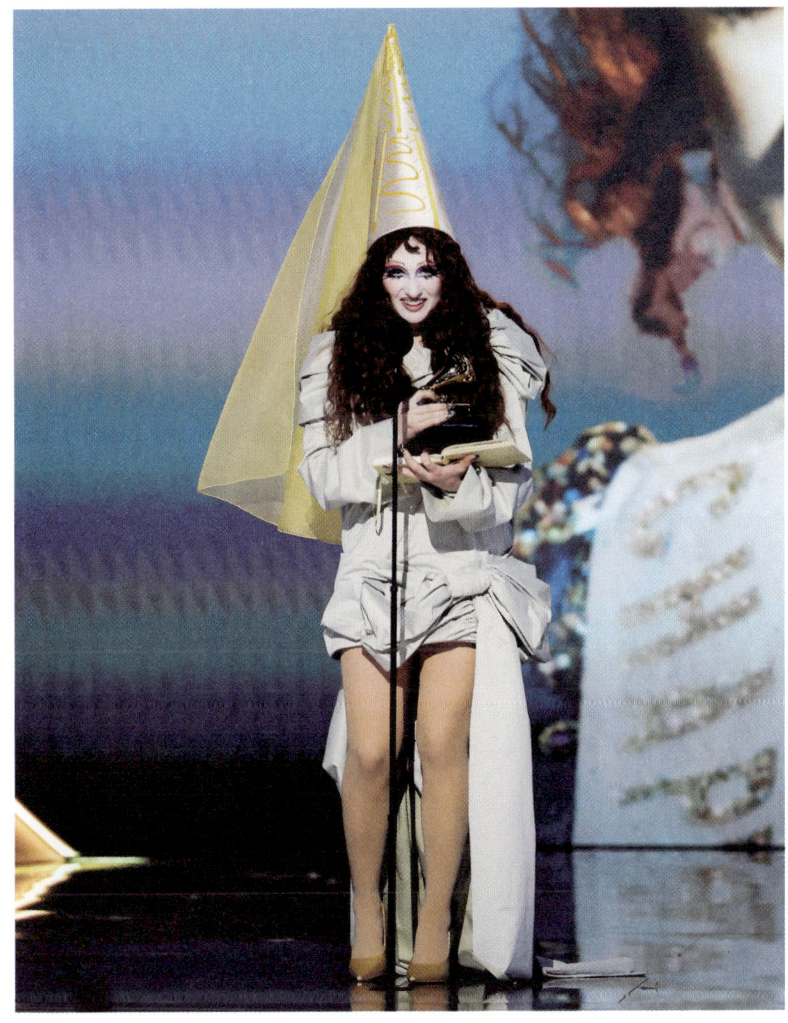

ENDNOTES

1. D'Souza, Shaad. 'Chappell Roan, pop's next big thing: "I grew up thinking being gay was a sin"'. *Guardian*, 29 December 2023.
2. Tonic, Gina. 'Chappell Roan on audience participation, playing a character and being horny.' Polyesterzine.com, 19 September 2023.
3. Fromson, Audrey. 'Chappell Roan on making pop music and giving back'. *Vanity Fair*, 18 September 2023.
4. Stone, Avery. 'A night out with Chappell Roan'. *Nylon*, 11 July 2023.
5. Solomon, Kate. '"Fame is like going through puberty": Chappell Roan on sexuality, superstardom and the joy of drag.' *Guardian*, 20 September 2024.
6. Spanos, Brittany. 'Chappell Roan is a pop supernova. Nothing about it has been easy'. *Rolling Stone*, 10 September 2024.
7. Levine, Nick. 'Chappell Roan: the pop supernova who feels like one of the "Drag Race" girls'. *NME*, 5 February 2024.
8. D'Souza, Shaad. 'Chappell Roan, pop's next big thing
9. 'Exclusive Interview with "Chappell Roan"'. illustratemagazine.com, 19 June 2022.
10. Spanos, Brittany. 'Chappell Roan is a pop supernova'.
11. D'Souza, Shaad. 'Chappell Roan, pop's next big thing'.
12. Spanos, Brittany. 'Chappell Roan is a pop supernova'.
13. Clymer, Liam. 'The Michigan Roots of the Midwest Princess'. Pridesource.com, 15 August 2024.
14. Fromson, Audrey. 'Chappell Roan on making pop music and giving back'.
15. Savage, Mark. 'Chappell Roan is the freak, fun popstar you need to know'. BBC News, 10 April 2024.
16. *The Tonight Show Starring Jimmy Fallon*. 'Chappell Roan talks outfit inspirations, new album and your favorite artist's favorite artist'. https://www.youtube.com/watch?v=L94zTNhLnXo, 21 June 2024.
17. D'Souza, Shaad. 'Chappell Roan, pop's next big thing'.
18. Savage, Mark. 'Chappell Roan is the freak, fun popstar you need to know'
19. Ribner, Sonya. 'Slumber Party Pop: A New Authenticity with Chappell Roan'. Cherwell.org, 12 August 2022.
20. Visti, Cat and Liberty, Cami. 'Chappell Roan: Interview'. *Unclear Magazine*, 10 December 2017.
21. Ribner, Sonya. 'Slumber Party Pop'.
22. 'Chappell Roan tells fans how to pronounce her name correctly'. Celebrity Gossip Central, YouTube, 19 June 2024.
23. Levine, Nick. 'Chappell Roan: the pop supernova who feels like one of the "Drag Race" girls'.
24. Spanos, Brittany. 'Chappell Roan is a pop supernova'.
25. D'Souza, Shaad. 'Chappell Roan, pop's next big thing'.
26. Savage, Mark. 'Chappell Roan is the freak, fun popstar you need to know'.
27. Alter, Rebecca. 'What if I told you the song of summer 2021 is this stripper's delight from summer 2020?'. *Vulture*, 27 May 2021.
28. D'Souza, Shaad. 'Chappell Roan, pop's next big thing'.
29. Spanos, Brittany. 'Chappell Roan is a pop supernova'.
30. Fromson, Audrey. 'Chappell Roan on making pop music and giving back'.
31. Fromson, Audrey. 'Chappell Roan on making pop music and giving back'.
32. Levine, Nick. 'Chappell Roan: the pop supernova who feels like one of the "Drag Race" girls'.
33. *The Tonight Show Starring Jimmy Fallon*. 'Chappell Roan talks outfit inspirations, new album and your favorite artist's favorite artist'.
34. Roan, Chappell (@chappellroan). TikTok video, 10 February 2022. https://www.tiktok.com/@chappellroan/video/7062920633059003694
35. Cramer, Jude. 'Chappell Roan's kink is karma, and our kink is Chappell Roan'. intomore.com, 8 July 2022.
36. Roan, Chappell (@chappellroan). Instagram post, 28 May 2022. https://www.instagram.com/p/CeMt8UXPw_n/
37. Roan, Chappell (@chappellroan). Instagram post, 7 August 2022. https://www.instagram.com/chappellroan/p/Cg-OIzXPpab/
38. Roan, Chappell (@chappellroan). Instagram post, 18 August 2022. https://www.instagram.com/p/ChabnLDv1ps/
39. Cai, Delia. 'The femininomenal ascent of Chappell Roan'. *The Face*, 16 September 2024.
40. Nguyen, Kelly. 'Chappell Roan's big year', https://www.grammy.com/news/chappell-roan-big-year-interview-coachella-performance, 19 April 2024
41. Fromson, Audrey. 'Chappell Roan on making pop music and giving back'.
42. Fromson, Audrey. 'Chappell Roan on making pop music and giving back'.
43. Tonic, Gina. 'Chappell Roan on audience participation, playing a character and being horny.'
44. Nguyen, Kelly. 'Chappell Roan's big year.'
45. Stone, Avery. 'A night out with Chappell Roan'.
46. 'Radio 1 Interview Podcast: Chappell Roan'. With Sian Eleri. BBC Radio 1, 16 May 2024.
47. 'Radio 1 Interview Podcast: Chappell Roan'.
48. NPR Music. 'Chappell Roan: Tiny Desk Concert'. YouTube, 21 March 2024. https://www.youtube.com/watch?v=w4WiXKGCJhg
49. 'Radio 1 Interview Podcast: Chappell Roan'.
50. 'Radio 1 Interview Podcast: Chappell Roan'.
51. TIME magazine (@time). TikTok video: '#chappellroan shaved off her eyebrows after receiving praise from #eltonjohn'. 3 May 2024, https://www.tiktok.com/@time/video/7353672509734030638
52. Apple Music. 'Chappell Roan & Elton John: "Good Luck, Babe!", New Music and Songwriting'. YouTube, 25 May 2024. https://youtu.be/UhA_fSGEpYs
53. Spanos, Brittany. 'Chappell Roan is a pop supernova'.
54. Anbouba, Margaux. 'Chappell Roan on her first ever Coachella and the magic of make-up'. *Vogue*, 14 April 2024.
55. Roan, Chappell (@chappellroan). Instagram post, 29 May 2024. https://www.instagram.com/chappellroan/p/C7kJET3PVkE
56. *The Tonight Show Starring Jimmy Fallon*. 'Chappell Roan talks outfit inspirations, new album and your favorite artist's favorite artist'.
57. Wagmeister, Elizabeth. 'Chappell Roan may have had the biggest Lollapalooza set of all time'. CNN.com, 5 August 2024.
58. Moore, Asia. 'Chappell Roan's performance reportedly breaks attendance record at Lollapalooza music fest'. *Los Angeles Times*, 7 August 2024.
59. Roan, Chappell (@chappellroan). Instagram post, 3 August 2024. https://www.instagram.com/p/C-NnmIzMyR8/
60. Solomon, Kate. '"Fame is like going through puberty"'.
61. Nolfi, Joey. '*RuPaul's Drag Race* winner Sasha Colby introduces Chappell Roan as her daughter at the MTV VMAs'. *Entertainment Weekly*, 11 September 2024.
62. 'Radio 1 Interview Podcast: Chappell Roan'.
63. BRITs. 'Chappell Roan wins International Song of the Year| The Brit Awards 2025'. YouTube, 1 March 2025. https://www.youtube.com/watch?v=4ZRNfRIqIo0
64. BRITs. 'Chappell Roan wins her second BRIT of the night – International Artist of the Year| The Brit Awards 2025'. YouTube, 1 March 2025. https://www.youtube.com/watch?v=eEIL4_luMXE
65. 'Radio 1 Interview Podcast: Chappell Roan'.
66. Roan, Chappell (@chappellroan). 'Holy fuck, remember when I was in the lovely bones?'. TikTok video, 3 June 2021. https://www.tiktok.com/@chappellroan/video/6969358926554942725
67. Savage, Mark. 'Chappell Roan: "I'd be more successful if I wore a muzzle"'. BBC News, 20 January 2025.
68. Fromson, Audrey. 'Chappell Roan on making pop music and giving back', *Vanity Fair*
69. 'Radio 1 Interview Podcast: Chappell Roan'.
70. Fromson, Audrey. 'Chappell Roan on making pop music and giving back'.
71. Cai, Delia. 'The femininomenal ascent of Chappell Roan'.
72. Solomon, Kate. '"Fame is like going through puberty"'.
73. Savage, Mark. 'Chappell Roan: "I'd be more successful if I wore a muzzle"'.
74. Tonic, Gina. 'Chappell Roan on audience participation, playing a character and being horny.'

75. Richards, Bailey. 'Chappell Roan scolds VIP section for being "too cool" to do her "Hot to Go!" dance at Outside Lands festival'. people.com, 12 August 2024.
76. Cai, Delia. 'The femininomenal ascent of Chappell Roan'.
77. Francis, Katie. '"I'm just being honest," Chappell Roan confesses as she tears up on stage and admits she's "having a hard time" at concert'. The *US Sun*, 13 June 2024.
78. Spanos, Brittany. 'Chappell Roan is a pop supernova'.
79. Solomon, Kate. '"Fame is like going through puberty"'.
80. Summers, Joan and Mattel, Trixie. 'Chappell Roan is taking it'. *Paper Magazine*, 4 June 2024.
81. Rolling Stone (@rollingstone). '@chappellroan gets emotional talking about her symbolic outfit at #Govball'. TikTok video, 9 June 2024. https://www.tiktok.com/@rollingstone/video/7378635519770578219.
82. Delgado, Sara. 'Chappell Roan reveals she declined the White House's Pride invite during Gov Ball'. *Teen Vogue*, 10 June 2024.
83. Recording Academy/GRAMMYs. 'Chappell Roan wins best new artist | 2025 GRAMMYs'. YouTube, 3 February 2025. https://www.youtube.com/watch?v=Rx86h_KXk48

PHOTO CREDITS

Cover image: Mary Mathis for The Washington Post via Getty Images

p.8 Patti McConville/Alamy Stock Photo
p.10 Arnold Jerocki/Getty Images for Valentino
p.12 Jim Bennett/Getty Images
p.13 Lisa Dragani/Getty Images
p.15 Everett Collection Inc/Alamy Stock Photo
p.16 Kevin Mazur/Getty Images for Acrisure Arena
p.18 Dania Maxwell/Los Angeles Times via Getty Images
p.22 Vivien Killilea/Getty Images for GLAAD
p.24 Mary Mathis for The Washington Post via Getty Images
p.26 Jim Bennett/Getty Images
p.29 Kevin Winter/Getty Images for The Recording Academy
p.31 ZUMA Press, Inc./Alamy Stock Photo
p.32 Gary Miller/FilmMagic/Getty Images
p.34 Michael Hurcomb/Shutterstock
p.38 Christopher Polk/Billboard via Getty Images
p.40 Associated Press/Alamy Stock Photo
p.42 Ralph Arvesen/Shutterstock
p.45 MediaPunch Inc/Alamy Stock Photo
p.46 Jim Dyson/Getty Images
p.47 Mary Mathis for The Washington Post via Getty Images
p.48 MediaPunch Inc/Alamy Stock Photo
p.50 Jim Dyson/Getty Images
p.51 Dana Jacobs/WireImage/Getty Images
p.54 Sipa US/Alamy Stock Photo
p.56 Mary Mathis for The Washington Post via Getty Images
p.58 Mary Mathis for The Washington Post via Getty Images
p.61 Christopher Polk/Billboard via Getty Images
p.64 Axelle/Bauer-Griffin/FilmMagic/Getty Images
p.66 Newscom/Alamy Stock Photo
p.68 Gilbert Flores/Billboard via Getty Images
p.71 Michael Kovac/Getty Images for Elton John AIDS Foundation
p.73 Dania Maxwell/Los Angeles Times via Getty Images
p.74 Astrida Valigorsky/Getty Images
p.76 Nina Westervelt/Billboard via Getty Images
p.79 Larry Marano/Shutterstock
p.81 Josh Brasted/FilmMagic/Getty Images
p.82 UPI/Alamy Stock Photo
p.84 ZUMA Press, Inc./Alamy Stock Photo
p.85 Stephen J. Cohen/Getty Images
p.87 John Salangsang/Shutterstock
p.89 Francis Specker/CBS via Getty Images
p.92 Axelle/Bauer-Griffin/FilmMagic/Getty Images
p.94 Scott Kowalchyk/CBS via Getty Images
p.96 Mary Mathis for The Washington Post via Getty Images
p.99 Axelle/Bauer-Griffin/FilmMagic/Getty Images
p.101 Sipa US/Alamy Stock Photo
p.102 Alex Garland/Alamy Stock Photo
p.104 Associated Press/Alamy Stock Photo
p.107 Nina Westervelt/Billboard via Getty Images
p.109 Kevin Winter/Getty Images for The Recording Academy

Quadrille, Penguin Random House UK, One Embassy Gardens, 8 Viaduct Gardens, London SW11 7BW

Quadrille Publishing Limited is part of the Penguin Random House group of companies whose addresses can be found at global.penguinrandomhouse.com

Published by Quadrille in 2025

www.penguin.co.uk

A CIP catalogue record for this book is available from the British Library

ISBN 978-1-83783-442-6
10 9 8 7 6 5 4 3 2 1

Publishing Director: Kate Pollard
Commissioning Editor: Phoebe Bath
Text: Tara O'Sullivan
Designer: Stuart Hardie
Production Controller: Sumayyah Waheed
Colour reproduction by p2d

Printed in China by RR Donnelley Asia Printing Solution Limited

The authorised representative in the EEA is Penguin Random House Ireland, Morrison Chambers, 32 Nassau Street, Dublin D02 YH68.

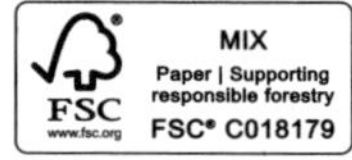

Penguin Random House is committed to a sustainable future for our business, our readers and our planet. This book is made from Forest Stewardship Council® certified paper.